Here's what peo_____ ____ __ HALFTIME:

This inspiring _____ ___ of a truly remarkable
individual and _____ r society—how to find
meaning and f_____ lives. In short, how to
move from suc_____

Stephen R. Covey
Covey Leadership Center

This is the book I am giving to my children.

Max DePree
Chairman, Herman Miller, Inc.
Author of Leadership Jazz *and* Leadership Is an Art

Halftime by Bob Buford is a radically personal, honestly engaging, deeply
moving, and spiritually challenging book. It confronts the reader with the
crucial choice between success and fruitfulness, death and life, fear and
love. It is a true call to conversion by a man for whom conversion has
become an ongoing way of life.

Henri Nouwen
L'Arche Daybreak

This book is for successful people who want more fulfillment in their lives
and realize it won't come from the next victory, the next sale, the next conquest, or significant increase in their bottom line. Let Bob Buford be your
guide to make sure your best years are ahead of you.

Ken Blanchard,
Co-author of The One Minute Manager

Bob's book challenges us to stop and think about the directions and priorities of our lives. Having struggled through the transitions in a life fully
examined and engaged, his insights and advice ring true and deep. His kind
of coaching, derived from having played the game with skill and grace, is
filled with wisdom that equips us with principles and strategies that enrich
our lives.

J. McDonald Williams
Chairman, Trammell Crow Company

According to Bob Buford, the first half of life is a quest for success, the second is a quest for significance. Bob should know; he has achieved the first
and is showing us the latter. You'll find this book to be unique, inspiring, and
practical. Read it and finish strong!

Max Lucado,
Author of When God Whispers Your Name

Bob Buford knows that in life, as in sports, it is important to finish well. What good are great stats in the first half if you come up short at the end? In a way success-minded Americans can understand, Bob gives a locker room pep talk on discovering life's basics. If you wonder if you have the right game plan for your life, call a time-out and read this book.

Stephen A. Hayner, Ph.D.
President, InterVarsity

Bob Buford is a friend and an inspiration. His life has not been limited to the usual or the ordinary. He has experienced both the pain and sorrow of loss and the joy of accomplishment. He has a vision for what could be and a focus on results. This book is a lesson in learning from a teacher who lives what he believes.

C. William Pollard
Chairman, ServiceMaster Company

Bob's personal story is an inspiring model for facing the huge challenges—and for grasping the unique opportunities—of life's second half.

Harold Myra
President, Christianity Today, Inc.

Bob Buford is one of those rare individuals who has made the transition from focusing on success to focusing on significance. This book will show you how to make the rest of your life the best of your life. I want every man in my congregation to read this inspiring story!

Dr. Rick Warren
Pastor, Saddleback Valley Community Church

Mr. Buford writes for the private chambers of the heart. For my part, just crossing forty, *Halftime* is received like a cup of cold water for a restless man, breathless at midrace but gathered for the final run.

David G. Bradley
Chairman, The Advisory Board Company
The Watergate

There are many rich young rulers who will be in heaven because of Bob Buford's life. Now he has created a brilliant work on how to stop counting the years and start making the years count. I know this will make my second half more meaningful.

Stephen Arterburn
The Minirth Meier New Life Clinics

Bob's approach really hits squarely at the feelings and the emotions in a way that possibly only a fellow Christian businessman, like Bob, can do.

Steven S. Reinemund
President and Chief Executive Officer, Frito-Lay, Inc.

I am someone who has benefited immeasurably from the second half of Bob Buford's life. He is one of the most effective kingdom catalysts I know.

Bill Hybels
Senior Pastor,
Willow Creek Community Church

For all who want to connect (or re-connect) passion with purpose, success with significance, and crowds with community, Bob Buford's words and life offer a graceful call to learn how to live what we believe. In the deepest and original sense, his is a "re-formed" life, a life that has been wonderfully shaped by his primary loyalty.

Don Flow
President, Flow Motors, Inc.

Halftime . . . presents some powerful ideas for a strategic plan for the rest of your life. Buford has a compelling concept that could throw huge new energies into projects that will make our communities stronger—and it will prevent us from coasting or burnout in the second half of our careers.

Merrill J. Oster
President, Oster Communications, Inc.

Bob's book makes us listen to those gnawing doubts we have about our approach to work and life; and then, in an easily-read style, gives us a way to analyze our options for doing better and for finding the courage to act.

Dennis Bakke
President, The AES Corporation

This is a book that should be read by people in both halves of their life. It is a book that I hope my children would read as they start their professional careers as a guide and road map for them to figure their lives out for themselves. It is a book that should be read and reread by those of us in or reaching the second half. It is a book that challenges the reader to action, and in taking that action, to greater service to themselves, their families, their community, and their maker.

Peter H. Coors
Chief Executive Officer,
Coors Brewing Company

Halftime is a fascinating story of spectacular success in business moving to spectacular significance in serving others. It holds not only Bob Buford's philosophy, but quotations from many wonderfully diverse philosophers on their spiritual journeys. It is a book for first and second-halfers and for all those who appreciate a warmly personal odyssey.

Frances Hesselbein
President and CEO,
The Drucker Foundation

I concluded a few years ago—as Bob Buford did—that "successful" was an inadequate epitaph. I wanted more from my life's journey. . . . I wish this book had been available when I began to address the very questions it explores. My pilgrimage led to significant, rewarding life decisions. The trip would have been easier with a road map like this on hand!

Bob Shank
Senior Pastor, South Coast Community Church

When you know a man has touched the peaks of success in what he does, been in the pit of intense grief and suffering in what he has experienced, and made the resolute choice to serve God with all he has and is, you want to read whatever he might write about his life and thoughts. You want to learn the secrets heaven has whispered to him, to know his soul and walk his path. This book will make all of that possible.

Gordon MacDonald
Senior Pastor, Grace Chapel ,
Lexington, Massachusetts

Bob Buford's *Halftime* is not only a powerful message; it's a spur to personal action. It's sincere and practical. It's moving and compelling. . . . I thank Bob for sharing his life story and his philosophy for a better tomorrow.

Michael J. Kami
Consultancy in Strategic Management

This is a book of great hope! Whether you are in the midst of an active career or are one of the many talented individuals whose careers have been prematurely sidelined, you will be encouraged by *Halftime*. Using biblical principles and his own fascinating experiences, Bob Buford provides every reader with the tools and inspiration to live a life of significance.

Kevin J. Jenkins
President & Chief Executive Officer
Canadian Airlines International, Ltd.

The best and most beautiful things in the world cannot be seen or touched, but are felt in the heart. This is what Bob Buford's book *Halftime* speaks about so eloquently!

Bruce Brookshire
Chairman of the Board,
Brookshire Grocery Company

HALF

*Changing Your Game Plan
from Success to Significance*

TIME

BOB BUFORD

ZondervanPublishingHouse
Grand Rapids, Michigan

A Division of HarperCollinsPublishers

Halftime
Copyright © 1994 by Robert P. Buford
All rights reserved

Requests for information should be addressed to:
Zondervan Publishing House
Grand Rapids, Michigan 49530

Buford, Bob.
    Halftime : changing your game plan from success to significance /
Bob Buford : foreword by Peter Drucker.
        p.   m.
    ISBN: 0-310-21532-3 (Softcover)
    1. Middle age–Religious life. 2. Middle age–Psychological aspects.
3. Self-realization. 4. Contentment. I. Title.
BV4579.5.B84   1994
248.8'42–dc20   94-41119
                                                                    CIP

Printed in the United States of America

Discussion guide prepared by W. Terry Whalin
Interior designed by Sue Koppenol

    98 99 00 01 02 /❖ DH/ 10 9 8 7

This book is dedicated to the two most important
people in my life:

To
Linda,
the woman who has shaped my heart,

and to
Peter Drucker,
the man who formed my mind.

CONTENTS

Foreword

This is a most unusual, indeed a unique, book—at least I do not know of any book that is even remotely similar.

It is immediately accessible as the autobiography of an unusual man and can be read as such with great pleasure. It is the story of obscure beginnings, the story of a boy who, barely eleven, after his father's early death, had to take on the burden of being the "man of the family"; a story of great hardships, of vision and determination, of sorrow and success.

While this in itself is interesting, what is unusual is that Bob Buford is one of the very few people I know who, still barely in his teens, thought through what his strengths were. This is something that, as a rule, only a few artists do. Even more incredible is that, when he realized that what the Lord had made him capable of doing well was very different from what he really *wanted* to do, he had the intellectual honesty and courage to say to himself, *It is my duty and mission to put to work what I am good at, rather than to do what I would love to do.* To this, of course, Bob owes his success as entrepreneur and businessman.

But—and this, in my experience, is truly unprecedented—Bob never forgot his original vision and never surrendered his original values to success. He refused to write off his youthful ambition as a child's dream. He kept his nose to the grindstone and yet never lost sight of the hills. And when, after thirty years of unremitting toil, he had reached the point where he could spare some time and some money, he then thought through again how to accomplish what he had wanted to do thirty years earlier, but to do so by putting his strengths, his experience, and his knowledge to work.

At this same point, many people retire. But Bob realized that he liked, indeed loved, his work and was very good at it. He knew that he should keep on doing what he was doing. But he also determined that the time had come for him to develop a parallel career in which his strengths, his knowledge, his experience—and his money—would serve his deep personal commitment to advance the Kingdom of God on earth; that is, to serve Christianity in his native land.

This is unusual enough. But at the same time, this book is far more than an autobiography. Without preaching, without trying to be "scholarly," without statistics and academic jargon, this book tackles the fundamental *social* challenge of a developed and affluent society such as ours has become.

Not so long ago, when I was born a few years before World War I, few people lived beyond what we now consider early middle age. As late as 1929, average life expectancy in the U.S. was not even fifty years—and half a century earlier it had been around thirty-five. But today the great majority of Americans—and of people in developed countries altogether—can expect to live twice as long as people could expect to live at the time of our great-grandparents.

Equally important, for the first time in history, a very large number of people can expect to be "successes"—something that, in the past, was practically unknown. Success does not necessarily mean a substantial fortune or even great worldly success. But it does mean attaining something that those in earlier times simply did not know: achievement, perhaps as professor in a college, as physician or lawyer, as a middle manager or professional in an organization or hospital administrator—all the jobs which, at the beginning of the century, either did not exist at all or were so few in numbers as to be socially insignificant.

Back then, work was a living, not a life. The worker in the steel plant, the farmer on the traditional family farm, the worker on the assembly line, the salesperson in the small mom-and-pop shop—all people in traditional employments—were perfectly ready to retire after thirty years, if only they could afford it. They did not miss their work, since it was never anything but a means to get their next meal on the table or to pay for the children's shoes.

Today, a growing number of people expect to find what Bob Buford found: that they enjoy their work, that they become better as they become older, that they are not ready to retire even though they may have the means to do so. A large and growing number of people—I call them "knowledge workers"—not only do much better financially than anybody in history has ever done, they do infinitely better in terms of personal fulfillment. And, yet, when they reach their mid-forties, the work they know and love is no longer challenging. They need new stimulus.

When I first became aware of this some twenty or thirty years ago, I thought that there would be an enormous number of "second career" people who would move from being, for instance, divisional controller in a big company to doing similar work in a nonprofit institution. I was wrong—Bob Buford taught me better. The great majority of these people do not want to leave what they are doing and what they are good at. But they do feel the need to add what Bob calls "the other half of their lives," what I would call "a parallel career." They want to find the sphere in which they can serve their values by putting to work what they're good at, using the strengths, knowledge, and experience they've already gained.

These are new challenges, unprecedented ones, as I said before. And this book is the first one, to my knowledge, that masterfully presents them and shows how to address them. This is pioneering of a high order. This is social analysis of a high order. And it is also a self-help book of the highest order. Whatever one's values and commitments—and they need not be at all those of Bob Buford—this book should be the catalyst for all those who are the beneficiaries of the two great social developments of this century: the extension of life span (especially of working life span), and the fact that it is now possible to be a "success" and to make a life out of one's living.

This is an important *political* book as well. We increasingly realize that modern government is not capable of taking care of community and social problems. Nor is the free market. There is a growing awareness of the need for a new sector—whether you call it "nonprofit," "third sector," "independent sector," or (my own preference) "social sector." In this sector, citizenship as a working "volunteer" once again becomes a reality rather than a ritual consisting of voting once in a while and paying taxes. Bob's book indicates the solution to the major political challenge of a developed society: that middle-aged success can help restore the body politic to function, to effectiveness, and to a reaffirmation of the basic values of both democracy and community.

This is also a *religious* book that goes to the heart of one of America's major challenges: the role of religion and Christianity in American society and in the life of America's people. Everybody knows that most of the mainstream churches in America have been steadily losing members in the last thirty or forty years. But what is amazing is not that the churches have lost members, but that they have lost so few! For the church membership of yesterday—and yesterday means only fifty or sixty years ago—was in a good many cases social compulsion rather than free choice.

When I first came to this country in the '30s as an American correspondent for a group of British papers, church attendance was mandatory. The application for a mortgage that we filled out within a few weeks of our moving to this country—and in an affluent and hardly "religious" New York City suburb to boot—asked for two references, one of whom had to be the pastor of the church you attended. If you had no such reference, you could not get a mortgage. Even twenty-five years later, in the early '50s, in small town and rural America somebody who did not go to church did not get a bank loan or a decent job.

This social pressure has now disappeared. But although we may have expected, as a result, a catastrophic decline in church membership, the decline has been modest by any standard—let alone by comparison with Europe —and it is being counteracted by the growth of the new, large "pastoral churches" that are growing in membership two or three times faster than the conventional churches are losing members. America, in other words, is still very much a Christian country, provided the churches learn how to serve today's constituencies: people who do not go to church because they are virtually forced to do so, but who go to church because they prefer it to everything else.

To have seen this early was one of Bob's great insights. His Leadership Network worked as a catalyst to make the large, pastoral churches work effectively, to identify their main problems, to make them capable of perpetuating themselves (as no earlier pastoral church has ever been able to do), and to focus them on their mission as apostles, witnesses, and central community services. And now he is extending this work to many churches, including midsized ones, not as a preacher but as an entrepreneur who converts latent energies into performance.

Finally, this book can—and should—be read as a story of growth from knowledge into wisdom, of intellectual and spiritual education. Such stories are rare indeed—and far more exciting, important, and instructive than swashbuckling adventure or "romantic" derring-do. These are the stories needed by those who have reached the middle of their life span, the ones who have become successful in the sense that they have achieved—just as the very young need the stories of heroic exploits and of romantic love.

This is, to conclude, a book that should and will be read on many levels. It is a book that will speak differently to different people. But it is a book that will have meaning and message for all those who open its pages.

Peter F. Drucker
September 1, 1994

INTRODUCTION:
Opening the Heart's Holiest Chamber

Then he told them many things in parables, saying: "A farmer went out to sow his seed. As he was scattering the seed, some fell along the path, and the birds came and ate it up. Some fell on rocky places, where it did not have much soil. It sprang up quickly, because the soil was shallow. But when the sun came up, the plants were scorched, and they withered because they had no root. Other seed fell among thorns, which grew up and choked the plants. Still other seed fell on good soil, where it produced a crop—a hundred, sixty or thirty times what was sown. He who has ears, let him hear."

Matthew 13:3–9

None of us knows when we will die. But any one of us, if we wish, may select our own epitaph. I have chosen mine. It is, I should confess, a somewhat haunting thing to think about your gravestone while you are vitally alive. Yet there it is, a vivid image in my mind and heart, standing as both a glorious inspiration and an epic challenge to me:

100X

It means 100 times. I have taken it for myself from the parable of the sower in Matthew 13. I'm an entrepreneur, and I want to be remembered as the seed that was planted in good soil and multiplied a hundred fold. It is how I wish to live. It is how I attempt to express my passions and my core commitments. It is how I envision my own legacy. I want to be a symbol of higher yield, in life and in death.

Saint Augustine said that asking yourself the question of your own legacy—*What do I wish to be remembered for?*—is the beginning of adulthood. That is what I have done by writing my own epitaph. After all, an epitaph should be something more than a wispy, wishful, self-selected motto. If it's honest, it says something about who you are at the essence of your personality and your soul.

The stuff that stirs within the heart's holiest chamber is, I believe, a gift given to us all by our Creator. It's one way of expressing a conviction that human beings are more than animals or machines. It is a confession that we are spiritual beings with a purpose—and a destiny. It's a divine reminder that we are miraculously and wonderfully made in the image of God.

You may call my 100X epitaph wishful thinking, and surely that is part of what it is. But when you select an epitaph as an expression of gratitude for your singular talent—and as a goal to which you are committed until you rest, at last, beneath the gravestone—you identify yourself as someone with a purpose and a passion that has been encoded in you for life.

The parable of the sower gets to the center of my dreams and to the kernel of my experiences. It is the driving force behind this book. My passion is to multiply all that God has given me and, in the process, give it back. And I would like to incite you to do the same. I do not want you to be the seed that fell along the path, or that was scattered in rocky places, or that was choked by weeds. Such seed held potential to become fruitful, but circumstances prevented it.

My own circumstances provided a moist and fertile soil in which I could grow. It was a fortunate environment, and that has been a critical factor in my story. My own tale is not that of the self-made man, nor is it a rags-to-riches account or a Horatio Alger fantasy. I was given far more opportunity for growth, personal development, and financial rewards than most Americans.

On the one hand you might say that I have been lucky, for indeed I have been given much with which to work. But if you believe, as I do, that "to whom much is given much is also required," you will begin to see how daunting my epitaph is.

What about your epitaph? What have you been given, and what will you do with it the rest of your life?

Recently I have begun looking at my own life through the metaphor of a football game (actually, any sport that divides its action into two halves will do). Up until my thirty-fifth year, I was in the first half. Then, circumstances intervened that sent me into halftime. Now I am playing the second half, and it's turning into a great game. Along the way, I have come to the conclusion that the second half of our lives should be the best half—that it can be, in fact, a personal renaissance.

During the first half of your life, if you are like me, you probably did not have time to think about how you would spend the rest of your life. You probably rushed through college, fell in love, married, embarked on a career, climbed upward, and acquired many things to help make the journey comfortable.

You played a hard-fought first half. You may have even been winning. But sooner or later you begin to wonder if this really is as good as it gets. Somehow, keeping score does not offer the thrill it once did.

You may have taken some vicious hits. A good share of men and women never make it to halftime without pain. Serious pain. Divorce. Too much alcohol. Not enough time for your kids. Guilt. Loneliness. Like many good players, you started the half with good intentions but got blindsided along the way.

Even if your pain was slight, you are smart enough to see that you cannot play the second half as you did the first. For one thing, you do not have the energy you once had. Fresh out of college, you had no problem with the fourteen-hour days and going in to the office on weekends. It was part of your first-half game plan, something almost inevitable if you hoped to succeed. But now you yearn for something more than success.

Then there is the reality of the game itself: The clock is running. What once looked like an eternity ahead of you is now within reach. And while you do not fear the end of the game, you do want to make sure that you finish well, that you leave something behind no one can take away from you. If the first half was a quest for success, the second half is a journey to significance.

The game is won or lost in the second half, not the first. It's possible to make some mistakes in the first half and still have time to recover, but it's harder to do that in the second half. In the second half you should, at long last, know what you have to work with. And you know the playing field—the world you live in. You have experienced enough victory to know how hard the game is most of the time, yet how easy it seems when the conditions are just right. You have experienced enough pain and disappointment to know that while losing a few rounds is certainly no fun, loss is survivable and sometimes uncovers the best that is in you.

Some people never get to the second half; a good many don't even know it exists. The prevailing view in our culture is that as you close out your fortieth year or so, you enter a period of aging and decline. To pair age with *growth* seems to be a contradiction in terms. This is a myth I refuse to believe, and I want to help you shatter it as well.

I do not know where you are in the game. If you are in your twenties, you have probably just received the opening kickoff and have an exciting half ahead of you. Much of what I write will seem far off to you, but do not put this book where you won't be able to find it later, for the first half races by faster than you think.

Most of you are probably nearing the end of the half. You are in your mid-thirties to early forties, and something has been telling you that you cannot keep playing as you have been. This book will speak most clearly to you.

Some of you may even be in the second half, but never really thought of it that way. Like a good lineman, you just kept charging ahead. This book may lead you to call time-out, head for the sidelines, and take stock, for it is never too late to change your game plan.

Regardless of where you are, I invite you, in the following pages, to discredit the view that the second half of your life will never measure up to the first. Instead of giving up and settling for life on its own terms, you are ready for new horizons, new challenges. You are ready to move from success to significance—to write your own epitaph—daring to believe that what you ultimately leave behind will be more important than anything you could have achieved in the first half of your life.

Part 1

The First Half

The real test of a man is not when he plays the role that he wants for himself, but when he plays the role destiny has for him.

Vaclav Havel

1

Listening to the Gentle Whisper

Then a great and powerful wind tore the mountains apart and shattered the rocks before the LORD, but the LORD was not in the wind. After the wind there was an earthquake, but the LORD was not in the earthquake. After the earthquake came a fire, but the LORD was not in the fire. And after the fire came a gentle whisper.

1 Kings 19:11b–12

I have not always paid attention to my life. To be honest, I only began paying close attention when I reached my early forties and found myself in a success panic. I was the president and CEO of a tremendously successful cable television company. I was fully engaged in a good and growing marriage. We had a son who was—there's no more appropriate way to say it—a prize.

And, of course, there was something gnawing at me. How was it that I could be so successful, so fortunate, and yet so frustratingly unfulfilled?

I knew perfectly well what I believed about business strategies and practices, family relationships, and the importance of friends. But I had not decided how I was going to reconcile all of these competing interests.

And, as for the most important issue of all, my life of faith, I knew *what* I believed, but I didn't really know what I planned to *do* about what I believed.

It was then that I started to wrestle with what I wanted out of the second half of my life. I was gripped with an unformed but very compelling idea that I should make my life truly productive, not merely profitable. I began to reckon with the implications of the seasons of my life and to listen for the sound of the gentle stillness that breaks forth, unexpectedly, after the fire.

I began asking myself questions like these:

- Am I listening for the still, small voice?
- Is my work still the center of my life and identity?
- Do I have an eternal perspective as a prism through which I view my life?
- What is my truest purpose? My life work? My destiny?
- What does it really mean to "have it all"?
- What do I want to be remembered for?
- What would my life look like if it really turned out well?

In the Scriptures, Jesus Christ preached that he had come so that his followers might have abundant life, life to the fullest. That's a wonderful sentiment. And I think its point is missed by many people who think that religion is restrictive and forbidding, who think that Jesus came to scowl and scold and say, "No!" The Jesus I had come to know and love was leading me to the paths of a large life, not a small or narrow one. He was asking me to say a loud "Yes!" to a life packed with significance.

But I did not hear his yes in my first half because I was too busy to listen.

The issue for me was not belief. I was given the gift of belief in God at an early age. But for most of my first half I was, to use a sports metaphor, stranded on second base. Consider the following diagram:

First base is taking the simple, childlike step of belief. For me, it was a simple acceptance that what Jesus said about himself in the Bible was true. This step involves what Kierkegaard called "a leap of faith." Faith doesn't deny reason, but it is different than reason. It accepts, as a gift from God, a different set of capacities. Without faith, we are spectators to affairs of the heart and soul. With faith, we can go on to engage the other two capacities, our rational and emotional senses, on the journey of personal growth to second base.

For me, the journey to second base was entirely about belief. It first engaged the heart and then the head. Rounding second base involved a shift from being what the Bible calls a "hearer of the Word" to being a "doer of the Word"—a shift from viewing faith as an internally held belief system to faith expressed in the form of loving behavior.

Faith expressed in behavior is "the most excellent way" Saint Paul speaks of in his great chapter on love, 1 Corinthians 13, which ends, "faith, hope and love." "The greatest of these is love," Paul says. The Greek word for love, *agape*, is exactly the same as the word for charity. Charity is the *expression* of love. It is as if faith and hope were acquired on the journey to second base in order to equip us for the second-half journey toward home base.

Third base involves becoming a follower by expressing our faith in the form of concrete work in a religious setting, either a church or a parachurch organization. And then we're finally on the last stretch, the journey to home base. This stage involves making ourselves what Gordon MacDonald has called Kingdom Builders. This means finding the mission in the world which has been specifically designed by God for each of us to do. It is what the Greeks called destiny, what poet John Donne referred to when he said, "No man is an island, entire of itself."

The second half of the baseball diamond is about good works. It is not at all separate from the first half, which is about belief, but grows out of that belief and gives it integrity. Paraphrasing Saint James' famous line "Faith without works is dead," I would put it this way: "Faith without works dies." The life of faith must become a life of individual responsibility. The legs and hands must follow the heart and the head, or the body is not whole.

While God would like to see all of us hit a home run, most Christians never get beyond belief. George Gallup Jr. says that 84 percent of Americans declare themselves to be Christians, which ought to be enough to infuse solid biblical values into all areas of culture. I do not doubt Gallup's findings, but I must tell you I do not see nearly that much evidence of Christian faith in our society. I believe that is because most of us are stuck somewhere between first and second base.

In the first half of life, there is barely enough time to go beyond second base. We are hunter-gatherers, doing our best to provide for our families, to advance our careers, and to pass our beliefs and values on to our children. In addition, for most men, and certainly a growing number of women, the first half finds us in our warrior mode. We need to prove to ourselves and others that we can accomplish something big, and the best way to do that is to become increasingly focused and intense.

I think of the first half as a season in which to develop faith and learn more about the unique way the Bible approaches life. The second half, when the pressure lets up, seems to be more the time when most people round second base and begin to *do* something about the faith they've developed. That's how it was for me.

In *The Odyssey,* the epic retelling of the life of Odysseus, there are two great forces pulling at Odysseus: work and home. He yearns to get home, yet he enjoys the battles along the way. Do you feel a kinship to him? During the first half, we too are pulled between the desire to be with our families and the adventure of trying to make it in our careers. Is it any wonder we do not hear that still, small voice calling us to something better?

The first half of life has to do with getting and gaining, learning and earning. Most do this in the most ordinary of ways: getting an education, entering the work force, starting a family, buying a house, earning enough money to provide for needs as well as a few wants, setting goals and climbing toward them. Some chase the prize in a more spectacular, aggressive fashion: winning through intimidation, acquiring through leveraged buyouts and mergers, doing whatever it takes to make it to the top. Either way, few leave time in the first half for listening to God. If we have any spiritual interests, they usually take their form in typical first-half fashion: serving on the church building committee, teaching a Sunday school class, or organizing the annual men's retreat.

The second half is more risky because it has to do with living beyond the immediate. It is about releasing the seed of creativity and energy that has been implanted within us, watering and cultivating it so that we may be abundantly fruitful. It involves investing our gifts in service to others—and receiving the personal joy that comes as a result of that spending. This is the kind of risk for which entrepreneurs earn excellent returns much of the time.

True entrepreneurship is not foolhardy, nor does it require particular courage. It merely seeks to gather and examine as many of the facts as possible about the market and the environment that might impact a decision. And then a decision must quickly be made. Likewise, for the second half of life to be better than the first, you must make the choice to step outside of the safety of living on autopilot. You must wrestle with who you are, why you believe what you profess to believe about your life, and what you do to provide meaning and structure to your daily activities and relationships.

There is a risk in this decision: In tossing aside the security blanket that keeps you safe and warm in your cautiously controlled zone of comfort, you may have to set aside familiar markers and reference points. You may feel, at least at first, that you are losing control of your life.

To which I say: Good for you.

It really is good for you to surrender control and, in the process, come more fully to your senses—those senses that enable you to be aware of life's adventures and its rewards.

Your future, particularly in turbulent times such as these, is in great measure beyond your control, no matter how hard you try to nail it down or plan it out. This is true whatever season of life you find yourself passing through. Yet, perhaps it is most resonant for those who are approaching their middle years, as I did within the past decade.

For me, the transition into the afternoon of life was a time for reordering my time and my treasure, for reconfiguring my values and my vision of what life could be. It represented more than a renewal; it was a new beginning. It was more than a reality check; it was a fresh and leisurely look into the holiest chamber of my own heart, affording me, at last, an opportunity to respond to my soul's deepest longings.

And it was, as it turned out, a time to plant and a time to uproot, a time to weep and a time to laugh, a time to mourn and a time to dance, a time to search and a time to give up, a time to keep and a time to throw away. It has been the most important time in my life.

So far.

Writer and director Norman Corwin, now in his eighties, recently recalled his transition into middle age in the book *The Ageless Spirit*:

> I remember now that the toughest birthday I ever faced was my fortieth. It was a big symbol because it said goodbye, goodbye, and goodbye to youth. But I think that when one has passed through that age it's like breaking the sound barrier.

For it surely is a time to discover, as George Bernard Shaw had some years before, a taste of the "true joy" of life. He described it this way:

> This is the true joy in life—the being used for a purpose recognized by yourself as a mighty one, the being a force of nature instead of a feverish, selfish little clod of ailments and grievances, complaining that the world will not devote itself to making you happy. I am of the opinion that my life belongs to the whole community and as long as I live, it is my privilege to do for it whatever I can. I want to be thoroughly used up when I die, for the harder I work, the more I live. I rejoice in life for its own sake. Life is no brief candle to me. It is a sort of splendid torch which I've got ahold of for the moment, and I want to make it burn as brightly as possible before handing it on to future generations.

In the introduction, I asked you to write your own epitaph to help you begin to think about your second half. Here's a question that will help you with the same goal:

If your life were absolutely perfect, how would it look to you?

That's something worth mulling over for a good while, because the picture that will emerge is a snapshot that will help you find your bliss, your blessedness. But it will be an accurate picture only to the extent that you listen to the still, small voice within.

2

The Hour of Reverse Conversion

Some Christians know the precise moment of their conversion. The date, the day of the week, the hour, minute, second, nano-second. Boom! In the twinkling of an eye, something happened, and they were changed . . . born-again . . . forgiven . . . saved.

That's not my story. I report this with neither regret nor pride. I was given the gift of faith at such an early age that I don't remember ever living without it. I have gone through my life with questions, to be sure, and the typical confusion about certain theological and doctrinal formulations, but I have never doubted God. I have always believed that Jesus is who he said he is.

I didn't achieve this state of trust and blissful assurance on my own. I didn't seek out the Lord. My unshaken faith is a gift from the Lord, the Lord who found *me.* So I can't recount a dramatic or emotional turning point in my spiritual development—save for a surprising, reverse conversion experience I had at the age of fourteen, at which time I abandoned the notion I had had of becoming a clergyman, although in no way did I renounce my personal faith or commitments.

By my adolescent years, my family had moved from Oklahoma to Tyler, Texas, in the piney woods on the eastern side of the Lone Star State. My father, who was a hard-drinking hunter and Oklahoma State Skeet Shooting champion, had died when I was in the fifth grade, before we moved to Texas. I don't remember a great deal about him, although I do recall that he drank his whiskey straight from the bottle, in a manner, I was to learn later, all-too-common during those postwar days when Ernest Hemingway was writing great American books and rugged American men thought themselves to be tempered-tough and indestructible.

My father was not indestructible.

He left a young widow and three small boys, and together we carried on. My mother continued running the radio station in Oklahoma for a brief time, and then we headed to Tyler, to purchase and operate a radio station there.

My mother, suddenly on her own, developed into a visionary and successful media business executive. She filed an application for a license to operate the first television station in Tyler, competing against the owner of the local newspaper and against the most prominent philanthropic family in town, whose business, of course, was oil.

The odds against her were daunting. She was a widow, alone and relatively new in town, while the family of the local oil tycoon provided money and leadership for virtually every community charity and cause. And in nearby Dallas, the three television licenses had been granted to the owners of the area's newspapers.

Meanwhile, my mother had to go to a court in Smith County, Texas, to have her "disabilities" removed. At that time, in the early 1950s, state law prevented women from executing and signing contracts without their husbands unless a court declared them "femme sole," a legal designation that literally means "woman alone."

But despite the odds, and in the face of considerable cultural roadblocks, my mother persevered and was granted the license to operate KLTV in October of 1954. (The "L" stood for Lucille, my mother's first name.) Her determination and doggedness provided an important lesson for me, giving me an example of a "can-do" spirit and belief. At an early age, I came to believe that I too could accomplish almost anything through hard work and persistence.

My mother, who subsequently remarried twice with lamentable lack of success both times, lived for her business interests and her children. When she tucked me in bed at night, she didn't read Dr. Seuss books or Winnie-the-Pooh adventures. Instead, she taught me about balance sheets, depreciation schedules, and advertising sales strategies. And when she applied for the television station license, she told the Federal Communications Commission that she was seeking to acquire a station in the hope that her children would one day run the business.

My mother's single-mindedness and dedication produced both excitement and tension within me—a titanic, internal tug-of-war between leading a life of success in business and leading a life of service in ministry. I would not fully resolve this tension for decades, but I made a decisive turn at the age of fourteen.

I remember the moment with crystal clarity, the same way some people remember every detail of the circumstances surrounding their conversion experience or where they were when they learned President John F. Kennedy had been shot.

My moment of vocational transformation took place in Miss Mittie Marsh's ninth-grade English class in Hogg Junior High School. Mittie Marsh was a legend in Tyler during my youth. She and her sisters, Minnie and Sarah, taught in the public schools in town and lived in a plantation-style mansion on South Broadway, the main street on which high school students cruised in their cars on Friday and Saturday nights. Mittie Marsh and her sisters set the standard for academic rigor in Tyler. They were the mentors who warned you, "If you don't get it right, you won't get into the college you want to go to."

I was seated in the second row on the far left side of the classroom. To this day I'm still not certain what prompted the decision, but it was in that spot that—Pow!— I somehow knew instantly that preaching, baptizing, marrying, and burying was out, and making money as a TV executive was in. I had made a clearheaded, teenaged decision to put myself in the driver's seat of a turbo-charged car.

Of course, "clearheaded" and "teenaged" are terms rarely seen on the same page, much less linked in the same clause, and television, then in its early infancy, scarcely looked to be a serious threat to the long-established American entertainment habits of reading, conversing, and listening to the radio. But what did I know? I was just in junior high, barely blossoming in the spring of my life. The world of business—and particularly the new and exciting technology of television—appeared to be a fabulous sport, with greater drama and spoils than I could imagine.

And, quite frankly, I wanted to be the guy who stepped to the plate and slugged the game-winning home run in the bottom of the ninth inning. Decisive. Heroic. It was a momentous choice that would pave the way for seasons still to come.

I still love the sport of the television business—the competition, the strategies, the conquests. One executive I knew (who later committed suicide) called business "the world's greatest sport." I know exactly what he meant, because I too once found it indescribably exhilarating to measure the competition, to run up the score, to win, win, win. I still find it enlivening to be a player of consequence. As well, I believe that human organizations provide the best learning environment and greatest intellectual challenge, much more so than memorizing facts from a book. What we learn formally is best enhanced through experience, and my experience in the television business has taught me a great deal about what it takes to be a winner in the success game.

But now I recognize that there are other games, played on many fields. And I've learned that there are ways to win besides dominating the ratings race and piling up the score through increased market share or burgeoning profits.

That valuable lesson was disclosed to me—as perhaps it already has been, or likely will be one day, to you—slowly, through uncomplicated attention-paying and the simple seasoning of the passages of life. It began to sink to my heart—and seep into the space where my decisions were being made—in significant ways about two decades ago, when I was doing great things in business, and little else.

It was the genesis of a steady and thoughtful reexamination of the stunning reverse conversion experience that had come to me in a flash in that junior high school classroom, where clearheaded dreams were launched in the fog of youth.

I began to think about what I would do about what I believed.

3

A Season of Searching and Self-Help

There is a time for everything . . . a time to search and a time to give up.

Ecclesiastes 3:1, 6

It's a cherished tenet of supply-side economics that a rising tide lifts all the boats in the ocean. Not everyone subscribes to that theory. But my industry, the television business, was nothing short of a commercial and cultural tidal wave that rolled across the United States during the 1960s and 1970s. It became an entertainment and information colossus, changing the way people behaved and related to each other.

My boat rose.

Walter Cronkite, the now-retired news anchor for CBS, emerged not only as a household name and familiar face, but "Uncle Walter" also ranked high on a list of the most trusted men in America. Because of television's power to confer authority and celebrity, that's the way it was—and largely still is.

It was, as you well might imagine, an especially fortuitous and rewarding time to be in the commercial television business. Over a three-decade period, in which my family's holdings expanded from a single TV station in Tyler to an array of cable television systems in several parts of the country, Buford Television, Inc., grew at a rate of 25 percent annually.

I learned many years ago from management expert Peter Drucker that for business growth to be sustained year after year, the leaders of a company have to be either crazy, crooked, or open to change based on their company's growth and the opportunities and challenges that expansion poses for them. Well, the television business gave us a wonderful ride from 1954 to 1986. Very few industries have had a period of uninterrupted growth like those of us in television management experienced during that time.

But the solid, even spectacular, growth of Buford Television, Inc., depended in some measure on judicious change. By the mid-1980s, for example, the action was no longer in owning individual stations. Most people in the United States had the option of watching thirty-five to fifty-five stations through cable linkup. At BTI, we divested our television stations and moved entirely into the cable business.

Business, like life, is seasonal. Circumstances change. A company, just like a person, needs to periodically shift its focus in order to achieve healthy growth.

I still recall the colorful early days of ABC-TV's "Monday Night Football" broadcasts, when "Dandy" Don Meredith, a former quarterback for the Dallas Cowboys, would signal to the audience that the game was done, even if there were several minutes remaining to be played. "Turn out the lights," he would sing in his Texas twang, "the party's over." Although I appreciate the wisdom in the old proverb that it's better to be lucky than smart, I believe that it's best of all to be bright enough to know when the party's over and when it's time to move on to the next event.

I moved into the presidency and chairman's seat in the company and became the oldest family member at the age of thirty-one, when my mother died in a fire that consumed her hotel room in downtown Dallas. My mother had taught me a great deal about business and about life. She was, like most people of achievement, a person of great strengths and also great weaknesses.

She was a risk-taker and forceful, dedicated to success in business and to raising me with the gifts of self-esteem and self-assurance. When I was in high school, she introduced me wherever we went as "the world's greatest left end." The truth was that I played on the second string in my junior year, backing up a truly fine, all-state left end. In my senior year, I started in that position, but was merely adequate as a football player. Still, I loved hearing her introduce me that way, and those words gave me both affirmation and inspiration.

But my mother was also naive and often undisciplined—weaknesses that no doubt contributed greatly to the disappointments and dissolution of her later marital relationships. They were weaknesses I swore to avoid.

Although I had worked in the family business since leaving college, my mother's death signaled a new season in my life—new responsibilities, new choices, new dreams. It was time for the next generation, and it came during an era of enormous upheaval in society. The leading edge of the baby boomers was entering college and the workforce. The Vietnam War was dragging on. Richard Nixon was plotting his reelection, and Watergate was waiting to happen.

I was not unaffected by all that social straining, but my chief focus was on growing the business and my self. I was deeply attracted to self-help and self-improvement books and tapes at the time. I read everything that Peter Drucker had written. I attended the American Management Association's Presidents' Course. I went to the Harvard Business School's Owner/Manager Program—a nine-week hothouse course that compressed major elements of their MBA curriculum.

Without benefit of the "mind-expanding" drugs that were popular at the time, I visualized my dreams. What I could conjure and believe, I knew I could achieve with a concerted effort of the will. That was my credo, my mantra. Tune out Woodstock and forget about White House dirty tricks and the trustworthiness of anyone over the age of thirty. I firmly believed I could shape my life by my dreams and the desires of my heart.

The only piece of my personality that gave me even a moment's pause was a fleeting concern about my degree of intensity and drivenness about the business. I had a sense that this hyperfocus might cost me in other areas of my life. Through all the excitement of actually running a business and reaping the rewards of success, a question tugged at a corner of my mind: *What might you lose with all this gaining?* Clearly, there was more to life than business.

Even so, not long after taking over the business, I hid myself away with a yellow pad and embarked on a painstaking career and personal evaluation that would allow course corrections.

I asked myself the question I posed to you in chapter 1:

If my life were absolutely perfect, what would its elements be?

I was thirty-four years old at the time, and it was the first opportunity I had taken in my life to reflect deeply on what I most wanted to accomplish and be. The answers would provide a glimpse of how I should live. I wrote down six goals:

1. To grow the business at least 10 percent a year.
2. To have a vital marriage to my wife, Linda, and to remain married to her until death temporarily forced us apart.
3. To serve God by serving others—to lay up treasure in heaven by teaching or counseling in my spare time at the church we attended, or anywhere else where I was allowed and encouraged to use my gifts.
4. To engender high self-esteem in our son, Ross. This, I believed, would best equip him for whatever circumstances he found himself in. I ranked myself as a father not so much on his grades or whether he won tennis tournaments, but rather on whether my son felt good about himself. An important part of this was instilling a grounded faith in something trustworthy beyond himself.
5. To grow culturally and intellectually, in ways that had somehow evaded me during my student years.
6. To figure out what to do with the money I was making and to determine how much was enough. I determined to invest the money I didn't use or didn't need in the highest cause I could imagine. What would that be?

These six goals were the way I made sense of what I was doing with my life. I focused almost exclusively on these areas and eliminated anything that didn't fit. The big change from my prior intense focus on growing the business was that I had introduced an element of balance into my life: The last five goals defined what was important to me. They answered the question, "What will I lose with all this gaining?" I wanted to be sure I didn't trade something I considered priceless—the love of my wife, the self-esteem of my son, the opportunity to broaden my horizons through learning, the expression of my faith through a life of service—for something I had come to have more than enough of: money, power, and achievement.

That was not, neither then nor now, an exhaustive list of life goals. But it was enough to get me into a search for the core commitments and passions that could help me make sense of myself.

I was a first-half player who was beginning to see the second half coming.

4

Success Panic

It snuck in like a thief in the night—a quiet, insidi-
ous intruder disturbing the dark peace and slinking about
to pick at the trappings of a life overflowing with contentment, money, achievement, and energy.

"Success panic" passed through the threshold of
my door when I was forty-four. It hit me with a blunt
object—my slavish devotion to the art of the deal and the
thrill of the kill. How much was enough?

By this time, the television business had grown
beyond our most optimistic projections. As a result, I had
long since arrived at—and, in fact, surpassed—the goals I
had established for accumulation of wealth. I had the big
house. I had the Jaguar. I could, and did, travel to any place
on earth I wished. I had either reached—or was ahead of—
the plan on most of the rest of my goals as well.

Success panic was wholly unexpected. I remember
reading a Sierra Club book about the assault on the west-
ern ridge of Mount Everest. After spending millions of dollars and experiencing loss of life among their fellow
climbers, two men finally reached the peak of Mount Everest. There, at the top, they viewed the world from its high-

est point. They had overcome enormous impediments to reach their destination, their ultimate goal, yet the emotion they experienced was not one of unadulterated elation and joyfulness. After just a few minutes, one of them began worrying about how to get down the other side before the wind blew them off the top of the mountain.

In the first-half mind-set, getting to the apex is far more exciting and rewarding than arriving.

When success panic struck, it brought me to a long-delayed crossroads and forced me to consider a critically important set of decisions before I could take another step:

- Would I move the finish line forward, so that I could keep running the race and measuring the time it took to complete each new lap?
- Would I give myself permission to be open to new possibilities?
- Could I have a constructive midlife crisis?
- After success, what?

These were difficult questions for me to address because of my attachment to business and my awareness of the entrepreneurial and leadership qualities that I had developed through my professional career. The business arena was the venue where I proved myself—my worth, my wisdom—each day; it was a stage on which I could demonstrate my gifts and my savvy. It was a comfortable world for me, not merely because it was familiar, but also because it was a world that expected me to be demanding and not loving. It was measurable.

I was, frankly, frightened by the idea of turning back toward the work of the church or works of service—those long-ago but not-quite-forgotten promptings toward ministry that had gripped me as a child.

Ministry—as I always had understood it—was loving, but not very demanding—the very antithesis of the real world I had populated quite cheerfully for nearly a quarter-century. It seemed too squishy, too nice, too other-worldly, too difficult to measure.

What's more, all my friends provided ample affirmation for me to remain as the CEO of a successful company. Yet, like Elijah, the still, small voice—barely audible, always gentle—kept calling to me as I was sitting there in a cold, middle-aged sweat brought on by the still-roaring flames of my success.

The gentle but insistent voice was asking me to consider—what else?—a question that I had deferred and suppressed for all of my adult life.

Do you understand the difference between being called and being driven?

Quite plainly, I had come to a point at which yet another fundamental decision had to be made. Like most decisions in real life, it was not a stark choice between black and white, between self-indulgence and self-denial, between leadership and followship; it would be found in the vast gray area between such polar extremes. But facing that question only served to underscore both the price and the glory of making a commitment to put my most central beliefs and tested talents into action in my life.

It was another helpful episode in my search for meaning, one that softened me up for the imminent exploration within, the probing that would finally help me unveil the source of my satisfaction and longings. For it was the question that made me wonder what I might be losing with all this gaining.

My worry was that I would become addicted to success. It's a delicate and dangerous zone—the interface between success and significance—to get as much success as you can without getting captured by it, becoming its prisoner. Keeping success the servant, not the master. It's a tension very much like the scene in *Fatal Attraction* where Michael Douglas is sitting across from Glenn Close, knowing that his wife is going to be gone for the weekend and feeling crazy with desire. He is right on the border between being master of his desire and committing an act that would make him its prisoner.

He chose to become a prisoner, and I knew it was time to make my own choice.

5

Locating the Mainspring

In my hour of deepest need, grace led me to an atheist. Mike Kami is a strategic planning consultant. He is brilliant. He is demanding. He is intuitive. He slices through all the pretense and posturing, and hones in on the core. A top resource consultant for the American Management Association, Kami was, at one time, director of strategic planning for IBM, serving that company during its years of rapid growth. He was then hired away by Xerox for a seven-figure bonus to do the same thing for them. He is independent, iconoclastic, and ruthless in his analysis.

He does not believe in God, but I can testify that—at least in my life—God worked unmistakably through Mike Kami.

I was accustomed to putting together periodic strategic plans for my business. These plans were a yardstick by which those of us in the company could measure our effectiveness in bringing our common dreams to fruition. They were easy to flesh out and, most of the time, fun to execute.

But this was substantially different. Now I needed to draw up a strategic plan for *me*. So I spread out my jumbled dreams and desires, lists of perceived strengths and weaknesses, professions of faith, projects begun and half-begun, things to do and things to abandon. It was a quagmire of both complementary and conflicting ambitions, a cacophony of noisy themes and trills of the sort one hears when symphony orchestra musicians are warming up for performance and seeking their pitch.

What should I do? How could I be most useful? Where should I invest my own talents, time, and treasure? What are the values that give purpose to my life? What is the overarching vision that shapes me? Who am I? Where am I? Where am I going? How do I get there?

In this blizzard of wonderment, Mike Kami asked me a simple and penetrating question:

What's in the box?

When I asked him to explain, Mike related an experience he had had with a group of Coca Cola executives and their plan to introduce "New Coke." The corporate leaders told Mike that the mainspring and driving force of their business was "great taste." They conducted numerous taste tests, found a new formula that tasted better than the original Coca Cola, introduced "New Coke" shortly thereafter—and promptly stepped into one of the biggest marketing debacles of all time.

They called Mike back in for another planning session. "You must have put the wrong word in the box," Mike told them. "Let's try again." After several hours, they found something else to put in the box: "American tradition."

The executives had recognized that pulling Coca Cola from the market was akin to tampering with an American institution like motherhood or apple pie. Finding the right word to put in the box enabled the company to recover its momentum quickly after a monumental blunder.

For my part, as I was searching for the right word to put in the box, I explained to Kami that I was open to fresh endeavors and new possibilities. I told him that I had gradually come to see that I really didn't have to be a religious professional or an ordained minister to live out my Christian convictions, and I warned him that I was serious about shifting at least some of my energy away from business pursuits into the direction of some unspecified realm of "service." It was probably a warning to me as well.

Well, Kami took me at my word. He announced that we could not put together an honest plan for my life until I identified the mainspring. "I've been listening to you for a couple of hours," he said, "and I'm going to ask you what's in the box. For you, it is either money or Jesus Christ. If you can tell me which it is, I can tell you the strategic planning implications of that choice. If you can't tell me, you are going to oscillate between those two values and be confused."

No one had ever put such a significant question to me so directly. After a few minutes (which seemed like hours), I said, "Well, if it has to be one or the other, I'll put Jesus Christ in the box."

It was an act of faith, and it was a daunting challenge to me to be open to change and adventure. Even more than that, *it was a commitment to do something about the faith I already had.* By acknowledging Christ as my guiding light, I had invoked the promise that he would direct my paths, no matter where they took me.

Our planning session was conducted at a beautiful spot in California. My wife, Linda, was with us so that she could be involved in the discussions and planning. Neither one of us knew fully what we were getting ourselves into, and both of us were considerably apprehensive.

Kami pushed us hard—and successfully. To put Christ in the box, I found, is actually a sign of contradiction, a paradox. To put Christ in the box is to break down the walls of the box and allow the power and grace of his life to invade every aspect of your own life. It follows the same wonderfully inverted logic as the ancient assertion that it is in giving that one receives, in our weakness we are made strong, and in dying we are born to richer life.

I had chosen to make Christ my primary loyalty, but not my exclusive loyalty. That was an important distinction, for I still had loyalties to Linda, to work, to friends, and to projects. Christ is the center of all that, but he would not stand in the way of those other things which give me balance and wholeness.

For me, the logic of this allegiance led me to stay involved with my business, functioning as a rear-echelon chairman of the board and devoting about 20 percent of my time to setting the vision and values of the company, picking key executives, setting standards, and monitoring performance. The remaining 80 percent of my time is given over to an array of other things, most of which center on leadership training for churches and nonprofit organizations—serving those who serve others, helping them be more effective in their work.

Let me be honest about this: I still have a penthouse in the city, a country home at the East Texas farm, and a new Lexus. I do not believe it is in keeping with my "calling" to assume a diametrically different lifestyle from the one I have enjoyed throughout my life. Many people avoid taking the risk for a better second half because they mistakenly think it necessitates a drastic change. But I believe God created us the way we are and enabled us to live the way we do for a purpose.

Related to this, what we *do* with what we believe grows out of our own history, and my history was neither missionary nor monastic. I truly believe that God uses people in their areas of strength and is unlikely to send us into areas in which we are likely to be amateurs and incompetents.

I realize that not everyone can afford to devote only 20 percent of his time to his career. In that respect, I am fortunate. But don't let the fact that you have to work for a living limit the grace God has in store for you during your second half. Don't allow the second half of your life to be characterized by decline, boredom, and increasing ineffectiveness for the kingdom.

Listen carefully to that still, small voice, and then do some honest soul-searching. What's in *your* box? Is it money? Career? Family? Freedom?

Remember, you can only have one thing in the box. Regardless of your position in life, once you have identified what's in your box, you will be able to see the cluster of activities—surrounded by quiet times for spiritual disciplines, reading, and reflecting—that put into play your "one thing" and keep you growing.

But be careful. Growth is not always easy.

6

"Adios, Ross"

There I was, sailing happily through my constructive midlife crisis, hoisting my "one thing" up the mast into
place, spinnaker billowing in the balmy breeze.

Then, without warning, along came a rogue wave
that blew the boat over.

I had gone through life more or less comfortable
with the idea that there are some things you know, some
things you suspect, and some things you're just never
going to understand. No less an authority than Aristotle
spoke to that when he said that the soul operates on two
levels: the rational, which takes in what can be seen and
measured; and the sphere beyond the rational, which
defies human comprehension and belongs in the realm of
the gods.

But this new development threatened to plunge me
into yet another dimension: the realm of the despondent.

My son Ross—our only child—was a person of
great promise. He was my heir, my successor, and, in ways
that may seem odd to you but absolutely real to me, one of
my greatest heroes.

After Ross graduated from Texas Christian University in Fort Worth, he moved to Denver to take a job as an investment banker. It was preparation for the time when he would come back to Texas to join the family business and eventually take a leadership position in it. He made $150,000 his first full year of work in the deal-making business, and his second year—only barely begun—would likely have sent his income soaring to over $500,000. There was big money to be made in his line of work in the late 1980s. But far more important than his financial successes, Ross was a good human being—determined, energetic, caring—with wonderful people skills. He had many friends, and he loved life in all its pleasures and ambiguities.

On the evening of January 3, 1987, I received a call from my brother Jeff, who told me that Ross and two of his friends had attempted to swim the Rio Grande River, which separates South Texas from Mexico.

"I think we have serious trouble," Jeff told me in a voice that meant it. "Ross is missing in the Rio Grande."

It was a lark that led the three young men to the Rio Grande: They wanted to experience what it was like for illegal aliens to cross the watery border into a land of promise. Ross was twenty-four years old, and it was the last adventure of his life on earth.

My brother informed me that the Texas Rangers were coordinating the search for Ross and one of his companions; the third young man was alive and frantic about the fate of his friends. I flew down to the Rio Grande Valley to join in the search, arriving by daybreak the next morning. I hired airplanes, helicopters, boats, trackers with dogs—everything that money could buy.

By three o'clock in the afternoon, I looked into the eyes of one of the trackers and knew that I would never see Ross again in this life.

I remember walking along a limestone bluff perhaps two hundred feet above the muddy and treacherous river, as frightened as I've ever felt. *Here's something you can't dream your way out of,* I told myself. *Here's something you can't think your way out of, buy your way out of, or work your way out of.*

It was all too clear in this maddening solitude on the river bluff. *This is,* I thought to myself, *something you can only trust your way out of.*

The incomprehensible was breaking out all around me, and there was no way I could understand it apart from an eternal perspective. Albert Einstein once said that "what is incomprehensible is beyond the realm of science. It is in the realm of God." This was truly in the realm of God.

I remember sending up a prayer that, in retrospect, seems to be the most intelligent petition I ever made to heaven. "Dear God," I pleaded, "somehow give me the ability to accept and absorb whatever grace people might bring to me at this terrible time. Amen."

The search for Ross and his friend continued, and grace abounded in my life and relationships. They found Ross' body in the spring, more than four months later, about ten miles downriver. Before his body was recovered, we had found on his desk at home in Denver a handwritten copy of his will, dated February 20, 1986, less than a year before the river swallowed his body. Through that long winter of fear and uncertainty, his words were also a grace to me.

"Well, if you're reading my will, then, obviously, I'm dead," Ross began. "I wonder how I died? Probably suddenly, because otherwise I would have taken the time to rewrite this. Even if I am dead, I think one thing should be remembered, and that is that I had a great time along the way. More importantly, it should be noted that I am in a better place now."

The will directed how he wanted his earthly goods distributed, and Ross concluded the document with this benediction: "In closing, I loved you all and thank you. You've made it a great life. Make sure you all go up instead of down and I'll be waiting for you at heaven's gate. Just look for the guy in the old khakis, Stetson, and faded shirt, wearing a pair of Ray-Bans and a Jack Nicholson smile. I also thank God for giving me the chance to write this before I departed. Thanks. Adios, Ross."

As horrifying and sad as it was, and is, to have lost him, Ross' disappearance and death also provided the greatest moments of rare insight and grandest gestures of immeasurable grace and joy that I ever hope to experience. Utter emptiness and brokenness left me feeling awful and wonderful at the same time. Close and silent embraces from friends, letters and phone calls of concern and empathy, and gifts of meals prepared and brought to our home were much-needed signs of love. One letter, in particular, showed us just how much Ross' life had been a witness to those around him:

Dear Mr. and Mrs. Buford,

Ross and I were best friends. All that he had, Ross shared with me. He shared his thoughts and ideas, his pleasures and his pains; he shared a whole lot of laughter. But most of all, he shared his love.

Well, now Ross has a new best friend. And now Ross is with his new best friend. But just as before, Ross continues to share. Today, Ross is sharing his new best friend with his old best friend.

I thank the Lord God for Ross, and I thank Ross for the Lord God.

Ronnie

Despite the comfort of those words, I was forced to lean on God entirely in those dark weeks after Ross' death, to think often of the Scripture verse "Trust in the Lord with all your heart, and lean not to your own understanding." I learned that God truly is sufficient and that his strength is made perfect in weakness. I learned that in my life on earth, I live as:

A pilgrim	not	In control
A steward	not	An owner
A soldier	not	With security

There is a simple Quaker prayer about giving and receiving that I uttered the night after I lost Ross and that I pray often to this day. Because the Quakers use their hands as a type of religious artifact or symbol, the first part of the prayer is done with your palms up, visualizing yourself receiving all that you need from God. The second part is prayed with palms down, visualizing all your cares and concerns being left in the lap of a benevolent and loving God.

I used this physical prayer when I spoke at a church two and a half weeks after we buried Ross.

"God," I began, "you have given my life into my hands. I give it back to you. My time, my property, my life itself . . . knowing it is only an instant compared to my life with you (and with Ross) in eternity."

With palms down, I concluded, "Father, to you I release the cares and concerns of this world, knowing you loved me enough to give your only Son in my behalf. I'm a sinner in need of a Savior and, once again, I accept what you have done for me as sufficient. In Jesus' name. Amen."

In his letter to the Romans, Saint Paul wrote a comforting message that has encouraged millions of troubled, despondent, broken believers over the centuries: "We know that God causes all things to work together for good to those who love God, to those who are called according to His purpose" (Romans 8:28 NASB). All things really do work together, but not without an eternal perspective.

I live in two worlds. One is the world of distraction and busyness. It's the world of deal-making and score-keeping, of stock market booms and busts. That world is like a cloud; it's going to perish. The other world I live in is where Ross is now—the world of the eternal. And it's the reality of that latter world that allows me to respond, with confidence: "Adios, Ross, *for now.*"

This eternal perspective has made me return, with soaring consolation, to George Bernard Shaw's eloquent passion for life and the responsibility to use it up each day. "I rejoice in life for its own sake," Shaw wrote. "Life is no brief candle to me. It's a sort of splendid torch which I've got hold of for the moment, and I want to make it burn as brightly as possible before handing it on to the future generations."

One reason I place my dear Ross on a short list of great heroes is because he was, despite the few years of his life, no brief candle. He was a splendid torch—vital, charismatic, magnetic, attractive—full of the attributes that all of us wish we had in greater abundance. Ross used his gifts to the full each day. He didn't shortchange himself, even though his days among us were so few. Ross' death, while tragic, was an inspiration to me to burn brightly while it is day.

John Donne, a famous English poet, once wrote, "No man is an island, entire of itself; every man is a piece of the continent, a part of the main. . . . Any man's death diminishes me, because I am involved in mankind; and therefore never send to know for whom the bell tolls; it tolls for thee."

Allow yourself to listen for the bell. And before it tolls for you, allow it to be your wake-up call.

Part 2

Halftime

The thing is to understand myself, to see what God really wishes me to do . . . to find the idea for which I can live and die.

Søren Kierkegaard

7

Taking Stock

I have often said that the sole cause of man's unhappiness is that he does not know how to stay quietly in his room.... What people want is not the easy peaceful life that allows us to think of our unhappy condition, nor the dangers of war, nor the burdens of office, but the agitation that takes our mind off it and diverts us. That is why we prefer the hunt to the capture. That is why men are so fond of hustle and bustle; that is why prison is such a fearful punishment; that is why the pleasures of solitude are so incomprehensible.

Pensees by Pascal

My father was a hunter. My son was a hunter, too. The genetic package that triggered the primal, outdoor, sportsman impulse within the two of them must have skipped a generational beat. I happen to be a gamesman, preferring sports whose results can be more readily measured and in which a time clock is either an ally or an opponent. I lean toward football, where you tally up statistics after each quarter, or the sport of business, where the bottom line is examined at the end of each quarter, too. At the end of both games, you have a final score.

I like keeping score.

Nevertheless, Pascal was right—many of us do prefer the hunt to the capture. We find greater satisfaction from the thrill of the chase than from the successful completion of the conquest. Burying ourselves in the hustle and bustle of daily existence, we rarely take time out to experience the wonder and stillness of solitude, where the quiet voice of God is most audible.

"If I were a doctor and were asked for my advice," theologian and philosopher Søren Kierkegaard once said, "I should reply: Create silence."

Halftime cannot be a noisy place.

The first half is noisy, busy, almost frenetic. It is not that you do not *want* to listen for that still, small voice. It's just that you never seem to have time to do it. Try to reconstruct your daily schedule from the past two weeks. Chances are, you will not even be able to remember what you did yesterday, let alone two weeks ago. If you pull out your datebook, however, you'll discover why—you simply had so many things on your plate it would be impossible to remember them all.

Were all of these activities important? Were they the types of things you would die for? Are you looking forward to more of the same? The expectation that work would provide more than a paycheck, that it would add meaning to life, has provoked an epidemic of dislocating and dispiriting midlife crises for many American workers. Millions of people enter their forties feeling not that they are at the pinnacle of their power or at the top of their career, but that they are trapped. Trapped in a job that rarely challenges them. Trapped in relationships that are stagnant, if not destructive. Trapped in the consequences of choices made a generation earlier.

There is an interesting workshop at Harvard Business School called Age of Options that is designed for people in halftime. The purpose of this workshop is to ensure participants "that their next career phase is fulfilling and imbued with purpose. It helps participants reassess their career development paths and define future choices in terms of personal needs and inclinations." I mention this not to promote their workshop but to emphasize how prevalent this need is in our culture. As the baby boomer generation begins hitting forty, there will be more and more people entering halftime.

It is not unnatural, nor should it overly concern you that you feel the need for a change. The mistake most people make when they begin to feel this way is to ignore the voice that is telling them to stop and listen. And there are many ways to ignore it. Some simply bear down, reasoning that they need more discipline, more focus. Some turn to diversions, both healthy and reckless. Most, I am convinced, enter a sort of sleepwalking stage where they force themselves to hold on until retirement. None of these approaches will make your second half better than the first, and may, in fact, make it worse.

If you are hearing a voice speak softly to you, it is time to head for the locker room, catch your breath, and get ready for the second half—a better second half than the first. For a football coach and his team, this is the time to take stock, to look back on what was accomplished. What worked? What didn't? Plays that didn't work will either be adjusted or dropped for the second half; new plays will be drawn up and inserted. Many times, a good second half depends on what is done during halftime.

As you take stock, ask yourself these similar questions: What is my passion? How am I wired? Where do I belong? What do I believe? What will I do about what I believe? Or, as Peter Drucker advises people who are looking for their life's task: What are my values, my aspirations, my directions, and what do I have to do, to learn, to change, in order to make myself capable of living up to my demands on myself and my expectations of life?

While I cannot tell you exactly how to answer those questions, I can share—in the form of general concepts—what worked best for me as I prepared to go back out onto the field.

Make peace. Too many people approach the second half of their lives with regrets over the first half. ("I should have spent more time with my family." "I should have developed better relationships." "I should have . . .") Regret is a tough emotion to live down: it haunts you in ways that will sap your strength and inspiration to go on to better things. So, one of the first things you need to do in halftime is make peace with your first-half set of issues.

This doesn't mean that you are proud of all you've done or that you would change nothing in your life if you could. Any honest look back will recall several things you wish you would have done differently. The key is to keep these things in perspective and accept them as an inevitable part of growth.

A friend of mine recalls having regrets about how he raised his son. He expressed those regrets to a family acquaintance and took great comfort in this reply: It doesn't help much to dwell on those things you did or didn't do in the past. At the time, you did the very best you could, given your knowledge and experience. You did not intentionally do anything to disappoint your son, even though now that you have the benefit of a few years' experience you can see how you might have done things differently. Don't blame yourself for good intentions that might have been applied improperly.

Since you cannot go back and undo past mistakes, you really have only two options. You can dwell on them and become consumed with the effects they may have had on your family and career. Or you can come to terms with them through grace, accepting them as poignant markers from which you can learn something valuable for the second half. Halftime is not about beating yourself up for what you did not do, but for coming to terms with your failures and recognizing that you live under grace.

Take time. The biggest mistake most of us make in the first half is not taking enough time on the things that are really important, so when you enter your halftime you need to make sure you don't repeat that mistake. Naturally, this requires a certain amount of discipline and time management, and there will be the tendency to view this as yet another appointment on your already-overscheduled datebook. But you would not be heading into halftime if you were not serious about making changes in your life.

A while ago I had the pleasure of meeting Konosuke Matsushita, chairman of the huge and highly successful Japanese electronics company bearing his last name. Matsushita follows the practice, not uncommon in Asia, of retreating to his garden from time to time in order to live a contemplative and reflective life. When Matsushita walks into a room, the awe is palpable. Without saying a word, he bespeaks a powerful centeredness and elegant reserve.

I am a big believer in getting away from the crowd for a period of time in order to do this kind of halftime thinking. It has become a distinctive of my second half—I set aside time for introspection almost every weekend. My few hours of uninterrupted reading and thinking are the wellspring from which I draw living water to nurture the activities of the rest of my week. For you, this could be anything from getting up an hour earlier and doing some quiet meditating to spending a long weekend at a hotel in another city.

It has taken you close to twenty years to get to halftime. Don't expect to solve all your first-half issues and plan for the second half in a few hours. For most people, halftime spreads out over several months, even years. But it will never happen if we don't give it the time it deserves.

Be deliberate. Halftime is more than putting your feet up and meditating. It's more than time away to think, pray, and play. A successful halftime needs some structure. Set an agenda that will help you "walk" through the important issues. Such an agenda will indeed include time to pray and listen, to read the Scriptures, and to think. But it should also include some deliberate questions. The following list may help you get started:

- Am I missing anything in my life right now that's important to me?
- What am I passionate about?
- Who am I?
- What do I value?
- What do I want to be doing in ten years? In twenty?
- What gifts has God given me that have been perfected over time?
- What gifts has he given me that I am unable to use?
- What would I be willing to die for?
- What is it about my job that makes me feel trapped?

- What realistic changes can I make in my employment?
- Would I be willing to take a less stressful (and less paying) job in order to be happier—to be closer to my true self?
- What steps do I need to take tomorrow in order to have a second half that is better than my first half?

You might consider writing your answers in a notebook or diary. I am engaged each day in writing a kind of spiritual autobiography—the sacred story of my very human existence, the relentless search for the most noble, decent part of me. If this seems a bit self-indulgent and prideful, it is because you still have one foot in the first half. Your "one thing" is still locked away in your heart's holiest chamber. Open your heart and let the answers spill out onto the pages of your own story.

Share the journey. I cannot imagine making the transition from the first half to the second without being accompanied on the journey by my wife. Linda was with me when I was forced to put either a dollar sign or a cross in the box that represented what was most important in my life. She did not flinch when I drew the cross, but she did not remain a silent partner. She asked questions, made suggestions, kept me honest. If your marriage is truly a partnership (which I believe it ought to be), it would be wrong for you to impose a whole new lifestyle onto your spouse without consulting her.

Be honest. Some people make the mistake of using halftime to fantasize, wistfully projecting various images of themselves into unrealistic situations that will never happen. In any other setting it's called daydreaming, and it's not a bad thing to do on your way home from work. But getting ready for a better second half is not daydreaming. You need to honestly face the tough, nitty-gritty questions about finances, other family members, long-range goals, etc. And when you *do* ask the hard questions, don't fudge on the answers. To make the second half better than the first, you need to discover the real you. For much of the first half, you had to be someone else. That's not duplicity, it's just the reality for all of us as we climb the ladder. Your second-half self is your genuine self, so be honest enough to discover it.

Be patient. It took you the better part of two decades to reach this point. You can't undo everything overnight. You will still have to go to work tomorrow. Bills will arrive in the mail. Clients will expect to have their calls returned. And a clear picture of what you should do with the rest of your life may not emerge anytime soon—or may not emerge at all.

Have faith. For Christians, halftime is basically a time to answer the question, "What will I do about what I believe?" Begin to answer that by putting faith to work, but trusting God to guide you. Listen to his voice through Scripture, and to the thoughts he places into your mind when you talk with him. To someone accustomed to listening to consultants, superiors, subordinates, and market research, this might be hard to do. Listen and trust.

HALFTIME DRILL

Answer the following questions to help you take stock of your first half as you prepare for a better second half. Be honest, and write down your answers.

1. What do I want to be remembered for?
   Write a description of how your life would look if it turned out just the way you wished.

2. What about money?
   How much is enough?
   If I have more than enough, what purpose do I
     serve with the excess?
   If I have less than enough, what am I willing to
     do to correct that?

3. How am I feeling about my career now?
   Is this what I want to be doing with my life ten
     years from now?

4. Am I living a balanced life?
   What are the important elements in my life that
     deserve more time?

5. What is the primary loyalty in my life?

6. Where do I look for inspiration, mentors, and
   working models for my second half?

7. Peter Drucker says that two important needs
   are self-realization and community. On a
   scale of 1–10 (10 being the highest), how am
   I doing in these areas?

8. Draw a line that describes the ups and downs
   of your life. Or draw three lines, one for
   personal life, one for family life, and one for
   work life. Where do they intersect? Where do
   they diverge?

9. Which of the following transition options
   seems to fit my temperament and gifts best?
   (Evaluate each option on a scale of 1–10.)
   a. Keep on doing what I already do well, but
      change the environment.
   b. Change the work, but stay in the same
      environment.
   c. Turn an avocation into a new career.

    d. Double-track (or even triple-track) in parallel careers (not hobbies).

    e. Keep on doing what I'm doing, even past retirement age.

10. What do I want for my children?

The purpose of halftime is to take stock, to listen, and to learn. It is the cry of the psalmist that resonates within the hearts of all who grow weary of the first half:

> Search me, O God, and know my heart; test me and know my anxious thoughts. See if there is any offensive way in me, and lead me in the way everlasting.
>
> (Psalm 139:23–24)

8

What Do You Believe?

I do not recall ever *not* believing in God, and I have a hunch (bolstered by many popular opinion polls) that most Americans also share this view. But for some reason, most of us seem stuck somewhere between disbelief and the quiet confidence that comes from knowing God. Why is that? Why did I spend so much of my first half trying to nail down what God was really like?

Part of this struggle with belief is a good thing. After all, God is at once simple and complex. The concept of an all-knowing, all-powerful, and personal Almighty is a pretty big package to wrap your arms around. The struggle with belief also comes from the very nature of who and what we are during the first half. In our best "conquering" mode, just as we chase the big deal or measure success by the size of our income, we may be unknowingly trying to add God to our list of achievements, or to quantify him. We study, analyze, dissect, and fathom until we can say, with great certainty and not a small measure of pride, that we have *acquired* God.

Here is where I believe the church has not been that helpful, for it seems to assume that those of us who sit in the pews and place our offering in the passing plates do not really believe. But the eighty million people who go to church Sunday after Sunday are there, for the most part, because they *do* believe in God. They are not atheists or pagan reprobates. They are God-seeking, if not God-fearing people who, unlike their secular counterparts, got up on a day off, put on a tie or a dress, and went to church. And most of them, once they get there, usually sit for an hour or more listening to a minister tell them things they already believe.

This can't go on forever. You can only hear so many sermons, attend so many Bible studies, and spend so much time looking inward. Halftime is the perfect opportunity to shift from trying to *understand* God to learning to *know* him. It is the time to humbly accept the fact that you may never fully understand him, but that you need to accept, on faith, that you are known and loved by him.

Jim Russell is a Michigan businessman who is clearly in the second half. After starting a business from the ground up and working hard to turn it into a very successful enterprise, he is now investing the lion's share of his time and energy into true second-half, kingdom-building work. As a way to get more Christians to do something with their belief in God, Jim established the Amy Awards writing contest. The contest is simple: Cash prizes ($10,000 to first place) are awarded to writers of articles that quote the Bible and support Christian teaching in secular newspapers or magazines.

Jim's goal is to encourage Christians to come out of hiding and take their rightful place in a diverse culture. His theory is that the proclamation victory has already been won—that is, the vast majority of Americans have heard the Gospel and have responded favorably—they just don't know what to do about their beliefs. And he honestly believes that once Christians learn what to do about what they believe, they could transform our nation. Pretty radical stuff from a conservative businessman, but his point is worth noting.

Sometimes I think we have complicated one of the simplest truths of the Bible: believe on the Lord Jesus Christ and you will be saved. These wonderful words of comfort do not necessarily mean that belonging to a church, having perfect insight into Christian theology, espousing the "right" position on church controversies, or giving to the correct charities will put you in a right relationship with Jesus. These things are not unimportant, but it may be time to ask yourself whether you are worrying too much about them. Then ask yourself: *Is this what I want to be doing for the rest of my life? Is this what faith in Christ ought to be all about?*

According to God's Word, becoming a Christian is an act of acceptance and belief. Accept Jesus as the Son of God and believe that he alone can save you from sin, and you are standing on first base. You do not need to wrestle with belief, because it is settled.

Do you believe? And do you believe so simply, with such childlike faith, that you are ready to put God completely in the box? Are you ready to get on with the second half of your life by moving beyond belief into action?

When I went to Mike Kami, I believed I was a Christian. After all, I had been given the gift of faith at an early age. But like many of those in the first half, my faith was very personal—something that was not quite ready to be shared. This insightful atheist forced me to settle the issue of belief in a dramatic and life-changing way by asking me to identify what was most important to me.

I have a friend who is a brilliant businessman—the kind of guy most would say has it made. He built a publishing empire around a simple idea, and in the process has acquired all the accoutrements of success. In addition, he has a lovely wife and a picture-book family, and is an active church member. Trim and fit and barely forty, he could retire tomorrow and enjoy the fruits of his success for the rest of his life. Instead, he is facing the real possibility of his wife leaving him. I know the situation well enough to be certain there is no "other man" in her life, and that he has been faithful to her. I also believe they love each other very much. But they are about to join the ranks of similar American family tragedies because my friend cannot bring himself to place just one thing in the box. In typical first-half fashion, he wants to have it all and is destroying himself and his family by trying to keep all the balls in the air.

You can only keep the box empty for so long. If you do not choose the one thing that belongs in the box, life's inertia will choose it for you. If my friend does not make a deliberate choice on his own, his business will force its way into the box. My guess is that most of the divorces that occur within the church are the result of letting something else decide what's in the box—letting circumstances settle the issue of how your belief is going to affect your commitments.

Do you see why it is important to settle this issue? In the first half, too many things were leading you away from the most important question in your life. You are in halftime because you do not want to go on any longer without finding the answer. The still, small voice has finally gotten your attention and you know you cannot return to the playing field without responding.

It's a question you *must* answer if you want your second half to be different—and better—than the first half of your life:

What's in *your* box?

9

Finding Your One Thing

Here is a parable from the Wild West as scripted by Hollywood. It is taken from what I consider to be the central scene in the movie *City Slickers*, starring Billy Crystal and Jack Palance.

Let me set the stage. Palance and Crystal are riding slowly across the range on horseback, discussing life and love. Palance plays a wily cowpoke, while Crystal is a tenderfoot from Los Angeles who has paid for a two-week dude ranch vacation. Of course, he gets more than he bargained for, and in the process, Crystal learns something important about himself.

Listen carefully to their slightly edited conversation:

CRYSTAL: " . . . and the second it's over, she's going to get back into her spaceship and fly away for eternity. Would you do it?"

PALANCE: "She a redhead?"

CRYSTAL: "Could be."

PALANCE: "I like redheads."

CRYSTAL: "You ever been married?"

PALANCE: "Nah."

CRYSTAL: "You ever been in love?"

PALANCE: "Once. I was driving a herd across the panhandle—Texas. Passed through this little dirt farm right about sundown. Out in the field was this young woman working down in the dirt. Just about then, she stood up and stretched her back. She was wearing a little cotton dress, and the settin' sun was right behind her showin' the shape that God had given her."

CRYSTAL: "What happened?"

PALANCE: "I just turned around and rode away."

CRYSTAL: "Why?"

PALANCE: "I figured it wasn't going to get any better than that."

CRYSTAL: "Yeah, but you could have been, you know, with her."

PALANCE: "I've been with lots of women."

CRYSTAL: "Yeah, but, you know, she could have been the love of your life."

PALANCE: "She is."

CRYSTAL: "That's great. That's ... not great. No, that's wrong, Curly. You passed up something that might have been terrific."

PALANCE: "My choice."

CRYSTAL: "I never could have done that."

PALANCE: "That's your choice. Cowboy leads a different kind of life. When there *were* cowboys. They're a dying breed. Still means something to me, though. In a couple of days, we'll move this herd across the river, drive them through the valley. Ahhh, (chuckles) there's nothing like bringing in the herd."

CRYSTAL: "You see, now, that's great. Your life makes sense to you."

PALANCE: (Laughs)

CRYSTAL: "What? What's so funny?"

PALANCE: "You city folk. You worry about a lot of s—, don't you?"

CRYSTAL: "S—? My wife basically told me she doesn't want me around."

PALANCE: "She a redhead?"

CRYSTAL: "I'm just saying . . ."

PALANCE: "How old are you? Thirty-eight?"

CRYSTAL: "Thirty-nine."

PALANCE: "Yeah. You all come out here about the same age. Same problems. Spend fifty weeks a year getting knots in your rope then—then you think two weeks up here will untie them for you. None of you get it. (Long pause) Do you know what the secret of life is?"

CRYSTAL: "No, what?"

PALANCE: "This." (Holds up his index finger)

CRYSTAL: "Your finger?"

PALANCE: "One thing. Just one thing. You stick to that and everything else don't mean s—."

CRYSTAL: "That's great, but what's the one thing?"

PALANCE: "That's what you've got to figure out."

When I first saw that scene, I recognized it immediately as a parable that uncovers a deep truth. It speaks to
the baby boomer generation with particular resonance,
and rings with authenticity and wisdom. Jack Palance, the
weather-beaten, wizened old philosopher with a Stetson
pulled low on his forehead and a cigarette dangling from
his lips, speaks the spare and sage words that are true for
you and me. They are not especially elegant words, but
they are eloquent in communicating a powerful message.

It's a sentiment remarkably similar to one voiced
by Eric Hoffer, the American longshoreman philosopher,
who shrewdly observed that "the feeling of being hurried
is not usually the result of living a full life and having no
time. It is, on the contrary, born of a vague fear that we are
wasting our life. When we do not do the one thing we
ought to do, we have no time for anything else—we are the
busiest people in the world." In the first half of your life,
you may have often felt you were one of the busiest people
in the world. The key to a successful second half is finding
your "one thing" and, in the process, finding what the
Bible calls a state of joy, or blessedness.

Most people never discover their "one thing." But
part of what is so unsettling about approaching the end of
the first half of our lives is that we know it is out there
somewhere. Like Billy Crystal's character, we desperately
long to find it, but we don't know for sure where to look.
Too often we try to fill that void with things that offer only
temporary relief:

- Making and spending money
- Projects and competition (winning)
- Relationships

Larry Crabb, author of *Inside Out*, refers to this
longing as a desire to fill a "hollow place located centrally

within us . . . the core desire of our soul." As you first began to experience success in your career, you satisfied this core desire by accumulating and gaining—remember, the first half is the hunter-gatherer mode. The proof is in your attic, garage, and closets! Note also how much time you devote to recreation, leisure, and social activities.

Are all of these activities bad? Of course you know they are not, but they will never satisfy that longing to find the "one thing" that is uniquely yours—the thing that, once found, will enable you to make a difference.

God has programmed your "one thing" into your life like computer software. Saint Paul writes about this in his epistle to the church at Ephesus: "For we are God's workmanship, created in Christ Jesus to do good works, which God prepared in advance for us to do" (Ephesians 2:10). Your one thing is the most essential part of you, your transcendent dimension. It is discovering what's true about yourself, rather than overlaying someone else's truth on you or injecting someone else's goals onto your personality.

Figuring out what's in the box will settle the issue of who or what will be the foundation of your life. It also settles the belief issue. But it's not enough to just identify what's in the box—you must also know who is holding it; who you are as a unique individual created for a purpose by God. What is your purpose? What makes you tick? What do you do so well that you would enjoy doing it without pay? What is your passion, the spark that needs only a little breeze to ignite into a raging fire?

We do not ask those questions during the first half of our lives because we are too busy doing what we think is right. But if it is beginning to seem as if the "right thing" is not your "one thing," you have reached the closing seconds of your first half. This is what Peter Drucker means when he teaches the difference between efficiency and effectiveness. Efficiency, Peter says, is doing things right. Effectiveness is doing the right things.

I would like to be more helpful than Jack Palance was for Billy Crystal, but finding your one thing really is your task. All I can tell you with any degree of certainty is that you will not find an abiding sense of purpose and direction by rushing from business appointment to church meeting to your son's soccer game to dinner with friends and then to bed. If you cannot afford to take the time and solitude before God that finding your "one thing" requires, you are not ready to find it.

10

From Success to Significance

There are two sources of unhappiness in life. One is not getting what you want; the other is getting it.
George Bernard Shaw

Why would Michael Jordan leave a game in which he was the dominant player on a world championship team and settle for a minor league spot on a second-rate team in another sport?

Why would John Malone take a 50 percent cut in pay to head up a struggling cable television system loaded down with thirty million dollars of debt?

And why are you scanning the want ads, looking at a possible career change, dreaming about owning a little restaurant, or maybe considering a short-term missions assignment?

One of the most common characteristics of a person who is nearing the end of the first half is that unquenchable desire to move from success to significance. After a first half of doing what we were supposed to do, we'd like to do something in the second half that is more meaningful—something that rises above perks and pay-checks into the stratosphere of significance.

Not that success is all bad. America is crazy about success, and for good reasons. From the earliest days of our youth we are encouraged to compete for the top prize, whether the contest is schoolyard tag or a classroom spelling bee. (I still, to this day, remember winning the first-grade spelling bee in Okmulgee, Oklahoma.) High school students study to achieve the highest possible rank-ing in their graduating class so that they will gain accep-tance to the top universities, which then put them on the right path toward a prized position in a prestigious firm. In turn, employers who gather enough of these front-runners hope to see their company's name at the top of somebody's "best of" list in a leading publication.

I have been in business thirty years and have yet to run into a company that deliberately tried to become sec-ond best. Nor should they. The drive to become the best is a powerful and positive motivator—it is the engine that drives not only a vibrant economy, but a whole way of life that treats excellence as though it is attainable. And even when we fall short of the prize, the effort has lifted us above our expectations.

The good life, in the most positive use of that term, is the result of a healthy desire to be successful. But on our way to becoming successful, we begin to pick up signals that tell us success isn't enough. You may be reading some of these signals:

1. The thrill of closing a major deal isn't quite what it was ten years ago.
2. A younger associate is nipping at your heels, and you respond by helping him rather than trying to stay ahead of him.

3. You spend a lot of time thinking what it might be like to start over or move "down" to a less responsible position that gives you more control of your life.

4. You have a secure position, yet you're scanning the want ads and openings listed in professional journals.

5. You wonder more about what makes a client tick, instead of how to sell him on a proposal.

6. You envy the guy who walked away from his job to spend more time with his family and that ministry work he's been dreaming about.

7. You use up all your vacation days and start taking some "comp time" as well.

8. You begin to ask yourself, "How much is enough?"

9. The boss's hint of a promotion doesn't motivate you as much as it used to.

10. You've been thinking very seriously about starting your own business.

11. Your son says one day, "Get a life, Dad."

Psychologist Donald Joy once observed that soon after a man turns forty, he is likely to tackle a huge undertaking—something that appears to be slightly out of his reach. If he's a farmer, he takes out a loan and expands the farm so that it is the biggest in the county. If he's a mid-level manager in an established company, he leaves to form his own business. Or he may try to make his mark in his hobby or avocation. A recreational rock climber, for example, may attempt to climb a major peak, or a Saturday sailor may try a solo ocean cruise.

Some may consider this ambitious push to excel yet another attempt to be successful, but it's more than that. As we move closer to the halftime of our lives, we realize that we can only buy, sell, manage, and attain so much. We also begin to understand that we will only *live* so long. When all is said and done, our success will be pretty empty unless it has included a corresponding degree of significance—and much of what we do in the first half is not imbued with the presence of the eternal. As one successful Harvard-educated businessman remarked about the many successes he had experienced in his business, "I was always finding out that beyond the pot of gold at the end of the rainbow, there's a sort of emptiness."

Consider my friend Howard. He's in his mid-forties and is the chairman, president, and CEO of his firm, the largest of its type in the city where he lives. He is also the most driven and compulsive person I know in an organization of high-powered, ambitious people called the Young Presidents Organization (YPO), to which I belong.

The trade press that covers his industry has called Howard "the Great White Shark" and has compared him to "a heat-seeking missile," descriptions intended—and taken—as compliments. The division Howard oversees is the crown jewel in a very large service industry holding company, and there is wide speculation that he will be asked to move to New York City to take the top job in the corporation someday.

Howard is a super success. I had dinner with him at a YPO meeting about three years ago, and he told me what accounted for his success.

"My career is what matters," he said. "I do four client dinners a week. I'm not home much, but my family has to understand that the job comes first. We get quality time on vacation, but that's about it for the year. That's just the way it is."

Then a rogue wave took a run at Howard. About eighteen months ago, he lost his only son in an accident.

There was nothing in Howard that prepared him for the loss of his son—absolutely nothing. He was grief-stricken and tormented by all manner of unanswerable questions. After the accident, when I saw Howard at YPO meetings, he would say quietly to me, "I'm not handling this very well. We've got to talk." Yet he didn't call. He poured himself even more single-mindedly into his work. But I could see in his eyes that something had snapped; his work wasn't working for him anymore.

Just a few months ago, I once again sat next to Howard at a YPO function. He leaned close and told me that he was staying on until the end of the year, but that his resignation and announcement of his hand-picked successor would appear in the next day's newspaper. He wasn't sure what he would be doing after that, but the thrill of the chase in business had absolutely lost its attraction for him as the full-time organizing principle of his life.

Then, with a broadening grin on his face, Howard informed me that he had spent the previous week calling his largest clients to inform them of his departure. "Something really strange happened during those calls," he said. "These guys are just like me, guys my age, hard drivers, tough, ambitious. I got virtually the identical reaction from each of them: First of all, I was greeted by about twenty seconds of pure silence, and then the guy would say, 'You son of a gun. You beat me to it. My wife and I have been talking about doing the same thing.'"

The last time I called Howard's office, he had skipped out to play basketball with inner-city kids at a recreation center. It was 10:00 A.M. on a weekday. His secretary said he would get back to me, but I told her there was no rush.

Howard had passed from the first half into halftime right before my eyes. He was discovering what was in the box.

Success often involves carrying your box with you as you head for the top, but never knowing what's in it. Significance begins by stopping wherever you are in the journey to see what's in the box, and then reordering your life around its contents. For the Christian, this may mean putting God in the box and then following wherever that decision leads. Unfortunately, most think a successful Christian businessman is a rich guy who gives a lot of money to the church. Significance comes when that businessman finds a way to give *himself* to God (if, indeed, God is in the box). That may or may not require a change of jobs, but it always requires a change of attitude. Dennis O'Connor and Donald M. Wolfe, in the *Journal of Organizational Behavior*, call this change in attitude a "personal paradigm shift (i.e., major changes in one's system of perceptions, beliefs, values, and feelings)." I sometimes call it a reordering of our personal myth.

For me, it meant handing over the day-to-day operation of my business to others so that I could be free to work directly with church leaders. That was my calling, the way I felt God was leading me to serve him. Before, I tithed from a substantial income and occasionally added to it with personal gifts; now I give approximately 75 percent of myself to causes that match up to the way God wired me.

You see, I don't believe that God creates us with specialized abilities and temperaments and then asks us to do things for him that require completely different abilities and temperaments. Why would a Creator who put together such an efficient and sensible natural world violate his design template when it came to man?

I recall an acquaintance who had a brilliant track record as a systems analyst. He was approaching halftime and wondered if there might be a way to devote more of his time and talent to God. The well-meaning pastor of his church "challenged" him to volunteer to teach a junior high Sunday school class! Nothing against teaching Sunday school (I've been doing it for years), but this guy could have been a valuable resource to the church through his computer and business skills. What he wanted was to move from success to significance, but he was offered a chance at almost certain failure. Which would you choose?

Significance need not be a 180-degree course change. Instead, do some retrofitting so that you can apply your gifts in ways that allow you to spend more time on things related to what's in your box. And do it in such a way as to reclaim the thrill of that first deal! God has a wonderful plan for the second half of your life: to allow you to serve him by doing what you like to do and what you are good at.

11

Finding the Center and Staying There

At the still point of the turning world. . . . There the dance is. Where the past and future are gathered. . . . The inner freedom from practical desire, the release from action and suffering. Release from inner and outer compulsion.

An adaptation of "Four Quartets" by T. S. Eliot—in calligraphy on the wall at Still Point Farm

I have always been drawn toward the center. Even in my first half—a time when most of us tend to flit frenetically between the anxiety of the chase and the boredom between deals—I was always able to somehow find my way back to the middle. I think I am just wired that way.

If my "centeredness" was a matter of luck in my first half, however, it is now a conscious choice. You can be lucky only so long. One of the warning signals of the end of the first half is the sense that you shouldn't spend too much time at either extreme. It is important to be deliberate about finding and holding in comfortable balance the creative tension that is the reality of life. Halftime gives us a chance to pause and identify the extremes between which we are caught, and then to determine how to live peacefully with them in the second half.

It can be done.

Harvard ethicist Laura Nash's instructive book *Believers in Business* is filled with stories of Christians living in the real world of the marketplace. For it, Nash conducted a study of sixty evangelical chief executive officers to discover how they balanced the competing tensions of their work.

First, consider the seven tensions she identified as common to Christians in the marketplace:

1. Serving God vs. pursuing mammon
2. Love vs. competition
3. People needs vs. profit obligations
4. Family vs. work
5. Keeping personal perspective in the face of success
6. Charity vs. wealth
7. Being a faithful witness in a pluralistic workplace

Sound familiar? Do you ever feel caught between any of these extremes? If you view these tensions negatively, you are probably still in the first half. But when you begin to see that these tensions are not only necessary but may have some benefits, you have entered halftime. In your journey into the second half, you will find ways to reduce the tension by learning how to deal with paradox. In other words, you will find peace in knowing that you will never resolve the tension—it will always be there, and there is nothing inherently wrong with it.

It sounds almost simplistic to report that Dr. Nash identifies two key words that describe how those sixty Christian CEOs positively handled these tensions: "balance" and "faith." If this sounds familiar, it is probably because the Bible has taught clearly that life is seldom an either/or proposition—that paradox is not bad. We learn this in the familiar passage of Ecclesiastes 3:

> There is a time for everything, and a season for every activity under heaven:
> a time to be born and a time to die,
> a time to plant and a time to uproot . . .
> a time to mourn and a time to dance . . .

And later:

> I have seen the burden God has laid on men. He has made everything beautiful in its time.

Saint Paul, too, speaks clearly of the "both/and" nature of life:

> Rather, as servants of God we commend ourselves in every way: in great endurance; in troubles, hardships and distresses; in beatings, imprisonments and riots; in hard work, sleepless nights and hunger; in purity, understanding, patience and kindness; in the Holy Spirit and in sincere love; in truthful speech and in the power of God; with weapons of righteousness in the right hand and in the left; through glory and dishonor, bad report and good report; genuine, yet regarded as impostors; known, yet regarded as unknown; dying, and yet we live on; beaten, and yet not killed; sorrowful, yet always rejoicing; poor, yet making many rich; having nothing, and yet possessing everything.
> (2 Corinthians 6:4–10)

That pretty much covers the waterfront, doesn't it? It was no different for any of the major Bible heroes—for Abraham or Joseph or Moses or David or the apostles—so who are *we* to expect comfortable, predictable lives? Instead, we are called to live somewhere in the middle of the tension and the paradox. And not to just exist in some spirit of tolerance, but to actually thrive! In athletics it is called the "zone"—that moment in time and space where the tensions of winning and losing, physics and the supernatural, man and spirit, are suspended ever so briefly for one game, one play, one hit.

Unfortunately, organized religion emphasizes a coming apart from chaos and confusion. (One pastor I know refers to the pulpit as being "ten feet safely above contradiction.") As far back as the Middle Ages, monasticism and religious orders have viewed religious life as a haven from the sin and hurly-burly of the streets. And today, we still view a serious religious life as something separate from the rest of the world—a career for credentialed professionals only.

In reality—a reality that the world needs to see—Christ meets us, he works with us, in the confusion, in the valley of the shadow of death, in the tunnel of chaos when the familiar landmarks have disappeared. And he is there with me on a ridge above the Rio Grande River, as I beat on the steering wheel of a rental car, wailing in grief over the loss of my son, tears and nosebleed raining down on my sweater, screaming out in pain at the horror of my loss.

He is there with me.

Modern man wants his life orderly and neat; his religion rational. In reality, however, we are suspended between the extremes of order and confusion, the known and the unknown. And only when we begin to settle our first-half issues and relinquish control over that desire to order our own lives will we be able to live comfortably in tension.

In my own pilgrimage, I have come to refer to this position of balance as the "J-Zone." On the extremes are anxiety and boredom. Neither is comfortable, nor is a life that finds us moving out of one and into the other and back again, over and over and over. Yet that is how most of us live in the first half.

It was only after I named what was in my box that I began to learn how to live comfortably with both anxiety and boredom. The closer I stayed to my center—Jesus—the more accepting I became of paradox. Anxiety and boredom were still there, it's just that I could now keep them at bay. I could be chasing down a major deal one day and reading Chaucer the next and somehow see how the in-between transcended both. In the J-Zone, I found that work and family are not either/or, that faith and the market do not exclude one another, that winning and losing are both okay.

Please do not mistake balance—the J-Zone—for success. To suggest that placing Jesus Christ at the center of my life resulted in overwhelming success would be dishonest and misleading. It has, however, quenched for me, as it will for you, the thirst for success by pouring the more satisfying draught of significance into the cup.

Let me give you an example. Soon after I met with Mike Kami and answered the question, "What's in the box?", I was confronted with a tremendous business opportunity. It was a delicious-looking deal, with a staggering potential payoff. As I pondered whether or not to jump in, I happened to be on an airplane bound for Washington D.C., and seated across the aisle from me was the head of a major federal agency, a man whose bureau would have a good deal to do with the very investment I was contemplating. As it happened, I knew him personally; he had been my lawyer before going to Washington.

I explained to him the opportunity and told him about my competing desire to serve Christ through my gift of entrepreneurship by allocating the majority of my time to a life of service. And then I asked him what he would do if he were in my shoes. Without hesitating, he said, "It seems to me you are standing on a mountaintop, and this is your temptation."

I asked this man if he was a student of the Bible and he replied, "Not really." But I knew that somewhere, somehow, he had drawn on a truth from the Bible. The first thing I did when I got to my hotel room was to search through the bedside Gideon Bible. Sure enough, what my friend was referring to was the second of the three temptations Satan put before Christ in the book of Matthew—the temptation for Jesus to do something spectacular, something that defied all the laws of gravity, something that proved that God had such special regard for him that he could defy natural law. The Tempter's voice says, "Go for it! This is your chance! Throw all your inhibition and caution to the wind! You'll never see this opportunity again."

The deal I was looking at defied several of the business world's laws of gravity. Although the return would be spectacular if it played out, it was a tax-driven venture in a business I knew nothing about. My inner voice said, "Life really isn't that easy. Stick to the things you know. Play out of the knowledge your experience has entitled you to possess."

Once again, someone who was not a particularly zealous Christian had led me to the deep truth that Scripture has for all of us. I became more convinced than ever that God uses all kinds of people to get us the help we need, if we will just be aware and sensitive. The man had seen clearly what I was perceiving only dimly. My conversation with him helped steer me back to my core, to my central values, from which I was tempted to stray. When I got back from Washington, I placed a phone call: the deal would have to be done without me.

In my first half, I would have considered that a deal I had lost. In my second, I accept it not as a win or a loss, but as one of those transcendent experiences in which I know and am comfortable with who I am and what I am here for.

If you find yourself yearning to respond similarly to a loss, maybe you are getting ready for *your* second half.

12

Staying in the Game, But Adjusting the Plan

My second half began when I walked away from my full-time, hands-on involvement with work. You probably cannot do that. But even if you can't, you can still have a second half.

By the time you get into halftime, your attitude toward your job may range from "I love my job so much I'd do it even if they didn't pay me" to "I can't stand what I do no matter how much money I make." I was lucky enough to be pretty close to the first response, but I realize there are many who are closer to the second. In fact, my hunch is that quite a few people do not like their job very much, and use it mainly as a means to an end.

I recall a young man who was a cold call, straight commission salesperson. He was one of those guys who didn't make a penny if he didn't sell something. No base salary. No drawing a salary on his commission. Just knock on doors and try to sell, and in this case, he sold fairly low-ticket items: notions and knickknacks to general stores and hardware stores.

But this guy was good: He sold enough to earn a six-figure income. That's a ton of knickknacks! Like most salesmen, he had a lot of drive and a lot of enthusiasm. In fact, he was so enthusiastic that I remarked about how much he must love selling. "I hate it," he replied. "But I love the pay." I mused to myself, recalling how my son, Ross, used to say, "I want to live to work, not work to live."

For me, my career demanded just those things I enjoyed giving, and it rewarded me with a great deal of satisfaction and with not a little money. To me, there was nothing more exhilarating than putting together a deal, negotiating the details, then celebrating after the handshake. I loved to develop a strategy to make the deal work. I was successful and received plenty of strokes, so it was not easy for me to decide to hand over the day-to-day operation of my business to a team of other people. In a sense, I was depriving myself of the pleasure I derived from my job.

Some people think that their problems would be over if they could just walk away from their job. In fact, this is one of the reasons why so many people stay in the first half: They get tired of the rat race and, instead of planning a successful midlife crisis, they jump ship. Change jobs. Start a business. Go independent.

None of the above are bad options, but I plead with you: Beware the urge to "get away from it all." That is not what the second half is all about. I know people who are well into their second halves who are still working at the same job they started with and who will be there to get the gold watch. The key to a successful second half is not a change of jobs; it is a change of heart, a change in the way you view the world and order your life. That might involve a completely new career or holding on to your present position. Usually, it is something between the two.

SEISMIC TESTING

Being from Texas, I can't help but have learned a few things about the oil business. I'm far from being an expert, mind you, but one of the things I have learned is that you don't just go out and pick a spot and start drilling. If you want to minimize your risks, you do some seismic testing—which is basically a sophisticated way to check out the landscape to see what it might produce. Since the size and shape of a subsurface formation is unknown, an electronic device is used to shoot sonar-like impulses down toward the formation from different points of view. The matter starts to take shape as it is seen from the various perspectives.

In terms of second-half seismic testing, your "subsurface formation" is that imponderable matter regarding how you will restructure your life. Your idea is indistinct in size and shape, and you can only see it from a limited viewpoint, so you go to six or eight different people you trust and ask them how *they* see it. Their "sonar" will reflect a part of the picture that you could not see before, and eventually the most vague and inchoate matters will begin to assume a definite size and shape. Then at least you know whether to drill or not.

You may think that once I decided what was in the box, I quickly handed the reins of my business over to a subordinate and walked out the door looking for new, albeit tamer, dragons to slay. Believe me, that would have been a big mistake, even though I was financially set for life and could afford some false starts. Instead, I did some seismic testing. I knew that I was gifted in the area of human organizations, and I also knew I enjoyed working in that area immensely. I could have stayed on in the human organization I had built, for I was assured continued success there, but I had already tasted success; it was significance I was after—something that got closer to both who I was and what was in the box. I did not see my cable television business as a primary source of significance in my life.

Neither did my adviser, Mike Kami. His advice was simple, and I wasn't quite ready for it: "Sell your company and invest the money in the ministry-oriented projects you've been talking about."

I sat there, stunned by the implications of this decision. Linda appeared no less stunned. I could almost see the stereotypical images of ministers, missionaries, and monastics passing through her mind. Would we be a philanthropic couple passing out money until our sack was empty? Would we be required to dress like a minister and his spouse? Had life as we'd known and enjoyed it come to a sudden, crashing, newly impoverished end?

Fortunately, I did some seismic testing. I sought the advice of two Christian leaders: Ray Steadman, then pastor of a church in Palo Alto, California, and James Dobson, popular author and founder of Focus on the Family. In their own way, each warned me: "If you sell your company, you will lose your platform and no one will return your calls." It was clear that I needed to be far more certain about where I was going with my life before I made any big plans.

So I called together a group of trusted advisers that included Fred Smith Sr., Paul Robbins, and Harold Myra of *Christianity Today*. Together, they had a broad overview and deep knowledge of the area in which I was preparing to work: the body of Christ in the United States. They knew how much I enjoyed working on organizational schemes, and that I wanted to spend a good share of my time on kingdom work. I asked them, "What are the opportunities for someone with my particular design?"

They reminded me of a new breed of churches that was very large and attempting to do church differently. "Maybe you could help them somehow," they suggested. So I invited a group of pastors together, asked Paul to serve as a nondirective moderator to ask them some questions, then sat back and listened.

Listening is a big part of seismic testing; it helps you discover areas of usefulness. I learned what these pastors perceived would be useful to them, and then continued my testing by facilitating focus groups of senior pastors from large churches. Eventually these pastors narrowed down their discussions to three things they felt would be useful to them, and I saw my second-half calling take shape.

As a direct result of this kind of testing, I was able to develop a network and support system that serves a unique group of people in Christian ministry. There is nothing magic about pastors of large churches; it just happens that, in God's providence, my interest in human organizations matched up nicely with their need to understand the dynamics of what is happening with their churches. If I was wired differently, I could have been hooked up just as easily with executives of overseas missions agencies or a network of small, rural churches. But had I rushed out of my session with Mike Kami and jumped at the first church-type job available, I probably would not have found something so closely aligned to who I am.

There are two keys to successful seismic testing. The first is to know who you are, and the second is to seek out reliable counsel. When I sought guidance from two friends, I asked, "What can I do to be useful?" They responded, "What does the 'I' consist of?" That's a very important question for anyone looking into the second half, because you cannot operate out of a strength that God doesn't give you.

Suppose you have often felt guilty about not doing enough evangelizing, so, when your second half rolls around, you decide to quit your job to become a preacher or a missionary. Instead, it might be much better to begin this decision-making process with a full knowledge and acceptance of who you are. Honestly assess your gifts and abilities. Is evangelism your gift? If it is something you enjoy doing and can do well—then do some seismic testing before you sign up for seminary or head to Africa. Assist your pastor on some calls to people interested in learning about Jesus or volunteer for a short-term missions assignment. If these brief explorations come back positive, then get more serious about what to do. If they come back negative, you will have saved yourself a lot of trouble.

What you do best for God will rise out of that core being he has created within you. Do you remember our Lord's parable of the talents? The wonderful message from this story is that you and I will only be held accountable for what we were given, not for what others might have or expect from us. The guy who was given only two talents and doubled them was esteemed as highly as the guy who started out with five. We are not all given the same equipment, but we are expected to know what we were given and find ways to invest ourselves wisely.

LOW-COST PROBES

I have a friend almost exactly my age who had come to a point similar to my own at halftime. He decided that God was the central, motivating factor in his life and that he wanted to find some way of giving his gift of leadership back to God. At about the same time, he was offered the CEO spot in a two-billion-dollar, highly leveraged company with operations ranging as far west as Thailand and as far east as Europe. It would be a tough, demanding, and challenging job with plenty of prestige and an annual salary approaching a million dollars. It was the type of position that people in the business community would die for . . . in fact, many do.

But if he took the job, he would be committed to at least five years—time that he had hoped to be spending in kingdom work.

He had also been thinking about going to seminary, so he came to me with these two choices: Fortune 500 or Hermeneutics 101. He had already made the decision to put God in the box, but he did not know whether that meant full-time, professional Christian ministry or something else.

I told him to take the CEO spot, forget about seminary, and to engage in some low-cost probes. To me, he had no choice. If he went to seminary, he would emerge three years later as a rank amateur at over fifty years of age. He might land an associate minister's job at a larger church and, by the time he was fifty-five, get a senior position at a church struggling to keep its head above water. Did my friend really think God gave him twenty-five years of training in business management and executive leadership so that he could pastor a medium-sized church struggling to find itself?

That did not mean, however, that my friend needed to disavow his allegiance to God. Low-cost probes involve practical explorations in the field or fields in which you think you would like to spend your second half. My friend, for example, may need to stay in the midst of international business, but look into starting an informal network of

Bible studies for other CEOs. It would take some phone calls, a few faxes, and a couple of trial balloons to show him if that is really a need, and if he's the one to fill it. Or, if he senses the need to eventually leave his career and work more in professional ministry, he might consider doing some consulting for Christian organizations—pro bono, if necessary.

My inviting a group of pastors to a meeting is another example of a low-cost probe. I had done my seismic testing by seeking out the counsel of trusted advisers who pointed me in the right direction, but I did not jump in with both feet. If that first meeting of pastors had fallen flat, my investment of time and money was such that I could have easily tried something else.

The point of low-cost probes is to gain some hands-on experience in combining your gifts with service to God and the church. It's done in business all the time in the form of market research, product testing, pilot projects, and the like. The reason people don't do it individually as they approach the second half is that they're still doing things the first-half way: full speed ahead with both feet. Remember, this second-half decision is about something more important than just another investment, just another sale. Slow down. Be deliberate. Test the waters.

THE HALF-SPEED OPTION

Let's say you really like your job and, frankly, you feel you need it. You need the security of a regular paycheck, health insurance, and pension, and you also enjoy the identity it gives you. You like being sales manager for Midtown Associates. Can someone like you look forward to a rewarding second half?

Actually, many people will fit this description. And the group really grows when we add those who don't necessarily like their work, but who find that leaving is not an option.

The good news is that people in this group certainly can have a second half that's better than the first. Let's face it. By the time you've been at something for ten to twenty years, you've pretty well mastered it. You've learned to delegate, you have a network of people who you know, you know the landscape, you've grown a productive list of clients, and you've found ways to get through each day without rushing at breakneck speed.

If you're really honest with yourself, you can probably work at half speed and still excel. That's what a lawyer friend of mine is doing. He is a senior partner in a very prestigious law firm who handles cases for some of the most powerful and famous people in the country. Scott (not his real name) loved what he was doing and was world-class at it, yet he sensed there was more to life than putting together megadeals—he sensed that he was missing something. There were second-half things he wanted to do, but he didn't want to walk away from a practice he'd worked so hard to build. Then he realized he could stay with his firm and still have time to invest himself in a very worthy project involving the public school systems around his state. Now when you ask him what he does for a living, he responds, somewhat facetiously, "I'm trying to convince my law partners that I still practice law." What he's really doing is taking half the time it used to take to drive his career and putting it into this new second-half commitment.

Or consider another acquaintance who's a public school teacher. He's one of the best science teachers in his state and would just as soon retire "in the saddle," but he too has some second-half goals to pursue. One of these is

to use his administrative skills to provide business leadership for his local church. He started out just like my lawyer
friend: hard-charging, working sixteen-hour days, push-
ing the envelope in order to become top in his field. Both
men love their work and do not feel it's time to leave it, so
they are using the additional time and energy that comes
from doing a good job at half speed to fulfill their second-
half goals.

You see, when it comes to having a better second
half than the first, it doesn't matter whether you're a mil-
lionaire CEO, a high-paid lawyer, or a teacher. What's
important is that you start off by discovering the way God
built you so that you can use your uniquely developed talents for him.

13

Overlapping Curves

It is one of the paradoxes of success that the things and ways which got you there are seldom those things that keep you there.

Charles Handy

Everything seems to conspire to keep us where we are. That is why so many people remain stuck in the first half or, at best, flounder in a perpetual halftime. Life seems more comfortable in known, familiar territory, even when we are fairly certain something better awaits us out there.

Take the Israelites, for instance. They were forever talking about the Promised Land, but they couldn't bring themselves to leave the familiar territory of Egypt. Not that Egypt was such a great place, but it was known; it had become home. For too many people today, the first half has become home.

I find it interesting that so many contemporary authors have recognized the stage of uncertainty that immobilizes people approaching midlife. William Bridges calls it the Neutral Zone. Scott Peck calls it the Tunnel of Chaos. Janet Hagberg calls it Stage 4: Power by reflection. Whatever its name, it is a zone that must be traversed in order to get to the promised land of the second half.

Many people don't make it through this zone, which is characterized by the pain of loss of former certainties and by confusion about what comes next. Graphically, it looks like this:

Seeing this time of uncertainty and sensing the pain, risk, and confusion involved in change, we have a tendency to cling to the known. The future seems to be somewhat fuzzy and vague, and doesn't compete well with the comfort and certainty of our present situation.

Then we can add to that fear of the uncertain these very real questions that haunt us:

- "How will I support myself?" (Own need for financial security)
- "How do you know this new idea will work? It sounds kind of iffy to me." (Rational friends)
- "What's going on here? This isn't the person I married!" (Concerned spouse)
- "Exactly what do you do, Daddy?" (Worried children)

In his very helpful book *The Age of Paradox,* Charles Handy captures this tension in a chapter entitled "The Sigmoid Curve." Handy sets up the problem with the sentence I quoted at the beginning of this chapter and repeat here: "It is one of the paradoxes of success that the things and ways which got you there are seldom those that keep you there."

Handy also offers a solution:

> The secret to constant growth is to start a new Sigmoid Curve before the first one peters out. The right place to start that second curve is at Point A (below) where there is the time, as well as the resources and energy, to get the new curve through its initial explorations and flounderings before the first curve begins to dip downward.

The Sigmoid Curve *Charles Handy The Age of Paradox*

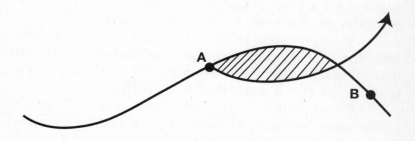

The normal pattern for most people is a single curve that rises as we approach middle age, then sharply falls off toward retirement. What Handy recommends is to start a new curve, preferably while the first one is still rising, but certainly before it begins to fall.

Ideally, life should consist of a series of overlapping curves. In my business life, the overlapping curves went something like this:

Before the first curve is played out	*Begin the second curve*
school	apprentice work
apprentice work	doing work
doing work	leading work
leading work	doing ministry
doing ministry	leading ministry
leading ministry	portfolio of ministries

It is possible to get stuck in any one of these areas. I know people close to my own age who are perpetual students. They acquire degrees like I used to acquire television stations. Others I've known have gotten stuck as the curve of "doing work" began to fall off. Before they knew it, there was no new curve rising on the horizon.

It is important to learn how to enjoy and benefit from the success you worked so hard to attain *without* becoming addicted to it, without going past the inflection point in the curve when it turns sour. Handy's Sigmoid Curve shows us that everything, even the best things, go pathological beyond that inflection point. And it is the realization that they could become stuck forever—"in a rut," as some say—that helps motivate some people to escape the first half.

Part of the key to getting to the second half is the marketing slogan a certain shoe company used to use: "Just do it!" But it is more than that. It is "doing it" at the right time, before your own first curve is picking up speed on the downturn. I know too many people who heard the still, small voice telling them to move on to something better, only to hold the advice at arm's length. They realized, of course, that the voice was true, but they also knew that to follow it would lead into unfamiliar, uncharted territory. *Better to wait until I am finished with what I am doing,* they think. But by the time they were finished, it was too late. They were too tired. And the voice was too faint to hear anymore.

Peter Drucker tells me that retirees have not proved to be the fertile source of volunteer effort we once thought they would be. They cut their engines off and lose their edge. Peter believes that if you do not have a second or parallel career in service by age forty-five, and if you are not vigorously involved in it by age fifty-five, it will never happen.

If the voice is speaking to you now, do not look for reasons to ignore it. There will always be reasons to stay where you are. It is faith that calls you to move on.

14

Leaping into the Abyss

We must be doing what we want the world to be.
Mohandas Gandhi

On my desk at home is a plaque that bears a motto of deep importance to me. It says something both serious and playful—serious because of its face-value meaning, yet playful because it came from the hilarious movie *The Blues Brothers*. Here is what it says: "On a Mission for God."

In the movie, which starred Dan Ackroyd and the late John Belushi as a pair of crazed brothers—Jake and Elwood Blues—Jake tells his brother he's on a mission from God. Unlike them, I'm on a mission *for* God. But just like them, I'm willing to crash a few cars along the way, and I'm inviting you to come along for the ride of your life.

Up to this point, I have tended to focus on the reasons why planning a better second half will be good for you, for indeed it will. But there is a much better reason to search for ways to harness your gifts to God's kingdom during the second half of your life, and that is its eternal value. God has always promoted win-win situations for his children. What is good for his kingdom is usually better for us as individuals.

For most of your first half, you may have wanted to keep God in the center of your box, but he kept getting squeezed out. I do not consider that wrong as much as inevitable. The demands of life and the nature of youth together make it very difficult to understand the biblical truth that in order to appreciate the magnitude of your individual significance, you must also understand and accept how small you are. While the first half is all about gaining, which sometimes results in loss, the second half is more about releasing and relinquishing, which usually results in strength. You do not see that clearly when you are twenty-six years old.

I have hesitated, at times, to tell my story. I have been so uniquely blessed that I don't want anyone to conclude that only rich guys can have a better second half. Please remember that my second half is going well not because I have money, but because I swallowed hard and put one thing in the box. It was not easy for me to do, nor will it be easy for you, either. But *that* is what has made the difference.

People who hear me speak often ask me if there are some people who can never have a better second half. In other words, is it ever too late to have a second half? Is a second half only for the upper middle class and above? Is it only for men? Is it only a Christian thing?

I have thought long and hard about this and have concluded that anyone who has grown weary of his or her life can do something to change it for the better. Anyone. I confess that I do not fully understand the unique issues that women face, but I suspect that both women who stay home and those who work in other venues reach a point at which they ask themselves, "Is this as good as it gets?"

My answer to them would be much the same that I give to men: "No, there are better things that await you."

I am also certain that those who do not profess faith in Christ may also have a better second half. In fact, much of my reading on this subject is from people who probably are not Christians, or at least their material is not presented in Christian or biblical terms. Yet, most agree that success eventually loses its luster and that significance is what we're really after. The secular person generally finds significance in some form of altruism; the Christian simply has a biblical framework to define his altruism.

So that leaves us with the question of age. Is it ever too late to move from the first half to the second? What about someone who is in his sixties? Seventies? Eighties? As long as we breathe, it is never too late in life to discover a better way. The existential writer Albert Camus discovered this truth: "In the midst of winter I finally learned that there was in me an invincible summer." We find our orders and our compass within us. "The more you listen to the voice within you, the better you will hear what is sounding outside," noted Dag Hammarskjold. "I don't know Who—or What—put the question—I don't know when it was put. I don't even remember answering. But at some moment I did answer Yes to Someone—or Something—and from that hour I was certain that existence is meaningful and that, therefore, my life, in self surrender, had a goal."

I choose to believe that it is God who speaks quietly inside us—that it is he who put the question deep within. And when we answer yes, he reveals the meaning he has chosen for us to enjoy; he unveils the goal that he has been keeping for us all along. I love how Paul puts it in Ephesians 2:

> For we are God's workmanship, created in Christ Jesus to do good works, which God prepared *in advance* for us to do.
>
> (v. 10, italics mine)

In a real football game, you cannot leave halftime and go back to the first half. In life you can. Some do. Others stay in halftime, forever struggling to come up with a new game plan. Still others try to live in the first half but make repeated ventures into the second. They are in a sort of perpetual seismic testing pattern, looking over the ledge but never jumping.

It is time to jump.

In an earlier chapter I advised that you be patient. I hope you don't consider it contradictory to tell you not to be *too* patient. It would be a shame to come this far and then settle back into your first-half game plan. There really is so much more for you to gain by putting one thing in your box and then going for it.

Then why do we hesitate? I have never tried bungee jumping, but I think I know what it must feel like to be perched at the top of a tower and hear the jump master tell me it's time to take the big plunge. In fact, when Mike Kami told me what I had to do after I drew a cross in the box, I knew that the most exhilarating way down would be to jump. Anything else would be climbing back down the ladder to safer, more familiar ground. The jump would be scary, unfamiliar, and, yes, dangerous—but it had the promise of the unforgettable.

I did not want to jump, but I knew that it was time.

My hunch is that you too know it's time, so let me conclude this section with two brief stories—one about a man who knew it was time but decided to climb back down the tower; the other about a man who jumped.

Jim wanted nothing more than to grab the top spot of a major company. He was a real hard-charger who was used to winning, and within a few years he had worked his way up to become the CEO of a large company in Dallas. But the joy was short-lived. Shortly after he reached the top, he was forced to place the company in Chapter 11 bankruptcy. I meet with Jim regularly and, after the company crashed, he began talking about going into teaching or maybe public service. One foot was in halftime, and I could see that he was sincere about making some significant changes in his life. Today, however, he's working harder than ever in an executive job in another large company.

Jim heard the still, small voice say, "It's time," but he didn't listen. He could not bring himself to jump.

Jack was a splendidly successful businessman who had the gift of making more money than he could have ever used up in a lifetime. He loved his work, but as he approached his middle years, he sensed a desire to move from success to significance. His seismic testing and low-cost probes pointed him toward Christian ministry, so he began looking for a way to use his skills and abilities in that area. Over a period of time, he observed that some of his business contacts wanted to serve a higher purpose with their money, but just didn't get around to doing it because they didn't have a staff to seek out the opportunities. So Jack began a firm to serve large corporations and wealthy individuals who have the inclination to reinvest their funds in worthy causes, but not the time. Jack searches for new entrepreneurial ideas and funds them with the excess money generated by his clients. The donors remain anonymous, yet get the pleasure of seeing their money at work during their lifetime.

Jack was at the edge of the bungee-jumping tower, but jumped with confidence and is having the time of his life.

What's stopping you?

Part 3

The Second Half

If one advances confidently in the direction of his dreams, and endeavors to live the life which he has imagined, he will meet with a success unexpected in common hours. He will pass an invisible boundary; new, universal, and more liberal laws will begin to establish themselves around and within him; and he will live with the license of a higher order of beings.

Henry David Thoreau

15

Life Mission

What I really lack is to be clear in my mind what I am to do, not what I am to know. . . . The thing is to understand myself, to see what God really wishes me to do . . . to find the idea for which I can live and die.

Søren Kierkegaard

As I approached my middle years, I began to feel that the time was drawing near when I should address concerns and questions that seemed more in the realm of the eternal than the temporal. When I discovered my "one thing," I felt more than ever before in concert with what was intended for my life. I felt that I could, through grace and diligence, live up to the epitaph I had chosen: 100X.

But it is not enough to *feel* like doing something significant. The newly discovered resolve that comes when you place just one thing in the box will fade if you do not apply it to a related goal. Most likely, your first half was filled with good intentions springing from your core beliefs. You wanted to be a better father, husband, Christian, and community member; you wanted to leave a positive mark on the world. And you probably lived up to more than a few of these expectations. Yet, something was still missing. All of your good intentions somehow could not fulfill that subconscious desire to be more significant than successful.

You had the right instincts, but no delivery system.

Lately, many businesses and other human organizations have developed mission statements, vision statements, or credos that attempt to explain why their company exists and what it hopes to accomplish. When such declarations are well-stated, they are usually easily understood and very simple. A mission statement becomes, as a team of consultants once noted in the *Harvard Business Review,* "the magnetic North Pole, the focal point" for that business. Everything the company does points in that direction.

Developing a *personal* mission statement makes a lot of sense, especially for second-halfers. During the first half, you probably either did not have time to develop such a declaration of mission, or the mission statement you adopted really belonged to the company for which you worked. You did not own it, or at least not in the sense that is now possible in the second half.

You will not get very far in your second half without knowing your life mission. Can yours be stated in a sentence or two? A good way to begin formulating one is with some questions (and nakedly honest answers). What is your passion? What have you achieved? What have you done uncommonly well? How are you wired? Where do you belong? What are the "shoulds" that have trailed you during the first half? These and other questions like them will direct you toward the self your heart longs for; they will help you discover the task for which you were especially made.

Stephen R. Covey, author of *The Seven Habits of Highly Effective People,* suggests that in developing a personal mission statement, you should focus on what you wish to be and do, based on the values and principles that undergird all your beliefs and actions. "Whatever is at the center of our life will be the source of our security, guidance, wisdom, and power," writes Covey.

My own mission statement is very short, but yours may be longer. One of the best (and longest) personal mission statements I know of was written by Andrew Carnegie when he was thirty-three years old, about the same age I was when I wrote my six goals for life. Here is what he wrote in his journal as a road map for how he would spend the rest of his days:

Thirty-three and an income of $50,000 per annum. By this time two years from now I can arrange all my business as to make no effort to increase fortune but spend the surplus each year for benevolent purposes. Settle in Oxford and get a thorough education, making the acquaintance of literary men—this will take three year's active work—pay especial attention to speaking in public. Settle then in London and purchase a controlling interest in some newspaper or live review and give the general management of it attention, taking a part in public matters especially those connected with education and improvement of the poorer classes. Man must have an idol—the amassing of wealth is one of the worst species of idolatry. No idol more debasing than the worship of money. Whatever I engage in I must push inordinately, therefore I should be careful to choose that life which will be the most elevating in its character. To continue much longer overwhelmed by busi-

> ness cares and with most of my thoughts wholly
> upon the way to make more money in the short-
> est time, must degrade me beyond hope of per-
> manent recovery. I will resign business at thirty-
> five, but during the ensuing two years, I wish to
> spend the afternoons in securing instruction,
> and in reading systematically.

Well, it turned out to be three decades—not two years—for Carnegie's vision of a life of service to come to pass. Even so, in the end his contribution was at least a hundredfold more than his original plan called for. From the time he invested the fruits of his first career in building the steel industry until his death in 1920, Carnegie replanted 90 percent of his fortune.

To show you that not every mission statement must be as long and involved as Carnegie's, I'll share mine. I like to think of myself as a strategic broker—someone who has the skills needed to link problem identifiers with problem solvers. This is how I am wired, this is what I did with my cable television business, so my life mission necessarily relates to this role. My life mission is: To transform the latent energy in American Christianity into active energy.

This is what I do; it is how I want my life to count. It releases me to be myself—to use gifts that are already there. I do not have to become something that feels uncomfortable or strange. If your own mission statement fits you as well, it will be the right one for you. If it forces you into something that does not fit, it will be someone else's mission.

Closely aligned with your mission statement are your life commitments. One of the consequences of my transition into the second half is that I no longer organize my life in terms of goals. Instead, I now make commitments. These commitments also help me stay focused on my mission, and

I share them here not because they are especially profound, but because they might encourage you to develop a list of commitments for your own life mission:

1. The primary loyalty of my life is Jesus Christ. I am committed to fully put into play my gifts in service to him.
2. I am committed to a vital marriage until "death do us part."
3. I have committed the majority of my time and money to beginning and developing a series of overlapping ventures which release the latent energy in American Christianity.
4. I am committed to be an effective steward of the resources entrusted to my care.
5. I am committed to be a good friend to ten people.
6. I am committed to have a renaissance in the second half of my life.
7. I am committed to practice "altruistic egoism." (Altruistic egoism means gaining personal satisfaction by helping others. It recognizes self-interest as central to my human design, and it counts as greatest gain the goodwill of one's neighbors.)

Here's one last tip to help you determine your second-half mission. Peter Drucker suggests that these are the two most important questions in helping you discover the unique role God has prepared beforehand for you to walk in. The questions are:

1. What have you achieved? (Competence)
2. What do you care deeply about? (Passion)

The goal is to find something that fits within the boundaries of these two questions—something you're good at and that really excites you. You may be good at working with people, yet care passionately about solitude. If you sell out to the first, the other will work against you. But if you look deeply enough inside of you and are honest about *combining* your competence with your passion, you will find the mission that is best suited to you.

An excellent resource to help you discover your life mission is the book *What Color Is Your Parachute?* by Dick Bolles. An ordained Episcopal priest, Bolles began his journey with *Parachute* when he was let go by his church in San Francisco, probably the best thing that could have happened to him, though it must not have seemed so at the time. Over the years since it was first released, Bolles has updated and revised the book, and the current edition includes a section called "How To Find Your Mission in Life."

Today, tomorrow, certainly by the end of next week, set aside some time to spend with a pencil and a sheet of paper—maybe several sheets. Make lists: things to do in your second half, things you are committed to, slogans and creeds that reflect the true you, statements that combine what you believe with what you want to do with the rest of your life.

After you have made your lists, pray. Read what you have written. Reflect. Listen. Share what you have written with your spouse and with a small group of friends. Then put the paper away in a drawer. Pray some more. Listen a lot. Think about what you love to do most, and let these thoughts roll gently through your soul like lazy waves on the ocean. This is the stuff that you never took the time to do in the first half—enjoy it!

In a week or so, get out a clean sheet of paper. Write these words at the top:

My Life Mission

I think you know what to do next.

16

Regaining Control

Unless a person takes charge of them, both work and free time are likely to be disappointing.
Mihaly Csikszentmihalyi

A friend of mine who had been president of a large publishing company once sought out a world-renowned Zen Master. After unloading the tremendous business of his life onto the Master without provoking much response, he decided to be quiet for a moment. The Zen Master began to pour tea into a beautiful Oriental teacup until it overflowed the cup and spread across the grass mat toward my friend. Bewildered, my friend asked the Zen Master what he was doing. The Zen Master replied:

Your life is like a teacup, flowing over. There's no room for anything new. You need to pour out, not take more in.

There are two kinds of capital that each of us has to spend. Economic capital is the money and time for leisure that you earn by working. For the most part, it is spent on living requirements and luxuries. Social capital is the time, money, and knowledge that is available to reinvest or spend in the community that nurtures you.

While most people think of spending money in "the pursuit of happiness," the concept of social capital basically says that the Lord has issued to each of us a portion of time, talent, and treasure to be invested in pursuing instead, the first and greatest commandment, "Thou shalt love the Lord thy God . . . and thy neighbor as thyself."

The payoff for investment of social capital is blessedness. This shouldn't be surprising. After all, perhaps the truest and most practical of Jesus' teachings is that "it is more blessed to give than to receive." What a difference it might have made had Thomas Jefferson reworded the Declaration of Independence to read "life, liberty, and the pursuit of *blessedness!*"

One major objective of an effective halftime and second half is to create capacity. Referring back to the story at the beginning of this chapter, my cup too was running over. I needed to create capacity by recapturing the majority of my time and by converting a good portion of my net worth into liquid funds to be invested for social purposes. I needed to transform my economic capital into social capital.

If you have followed the mutual funds market, you are probably familiar with the name Peter Lynch. Peter is a terrific example of someone who transformed economic capital into social capital. As portfolio manager for Fidelity Investments' Magellan Fund, he took the fund from twenty million to fourteen *billion* in his thirteen-year tenure at its helm. He had it all. Great job. Great family. Great satisfaction from working with charities. Yet at age forty-six, he decided to put boundaries on the time he was willing to spend at his job so that he could assume greater control over his life.

Lynch had come to the realization that eventually overtakes all of us: *I can't keep living like this.* It's not that what he was doing was so bad. In fact, it was all very good. But, as he explained, "For me it was like hot fudge sundaes: How much can you handle without getting a stomachache?" He now leaves home at 8:00 A.M., after his kids leave. He works four days a week (two for Fidelity and two for charity), and Mondays he allocates entirely to his wife.

Most first-halfers become victims of centrifugal force. Around the perimeter of their lives are vital points that demand attention: family, work, community involvement (service clubs, local school, etc.), church, professional development, leisure activities, and avocations. They begin with every good intention of tending to each, but in order to do that, they have to shift into a higher gear. Before long, they are spinning rapidly around the perimeter, the resulting force driving them farther and farther from the center, the core of who they are. At that point, all control has been lost.

The second half is about regaining control of your life—about calling your own shots. Do you think it was easy for Peter Lynch to tell his colleagues at Fidelity Investments that he was no longer going to manage their most profitable and visible fund? He was able to do it because he knew that being unable to control his work life would sooner or later result in a major loss in the other important areas of his life.

Getting back to the center requires us to downshift, to slow down. And once we return to the core—once we know who we are and what's in the box—we can accept the fact that some of the things on the perimeter will not receive as much attention as they once did. Some things will be more important than others; some may need to be ignored altogether. But regardless of what stays and what gets tossed aside, the point is that we no longer let some-one else decide that for us. We create capacity for the things that matter.

If this sounds radical or out of step with the way things generally work, it is because we are the first genera-tion to enjoy the luxury of choosing what we do with our second half. Your parents were probably very much like my father-in-law, who worked as a senior executive with an international oil supply company until he retired. It was important for him to stay the course in order to get the med-ical, dental, and postretirement benefits that come with long service to a large, hierarchical company. As well, most people in our parents' generation had what author Charles Handy calls "employment work": full-time, salary jobs with attractive benefits packages in good-sized companies.

That's not the way it's going to be in the future. Every day, newspapers report how big companies are lay-ing off more and more people—both blue- and white-collar workers. "Downsizing," "rightsizing," and "reengineering" are the current buzzwords of the corporate environment. Most job growth today is in firms who have fewer than one hundred employees—a great part of the growth in firms with fewer than twenty employees! Peter Drucker believes that one of the major reasons for the growth of these smaller firms is that a man can be his own boss and call more of his own shots.

In his book *The Age of Unreason,* Charles Handy asserts that in the future people will spend only about half of their working hours in employment organizations, with the remaining half spent in what he calls "portfolio work" —part-time work, consulting work, and temporary work for a variety of employers. My cable television company, for example, built 4,500 miles of cable television in about two years, using almost entirely small-firm subcontractors to obtain the franchises, map the systems, construct the cable, market the subscribers, and get them installed.

All of these trends make it increasingly possible for anyone to make the changes that are necessary in order to have a significant second half. People will be freer to choose what they do than ever before, allowing them to discard the work-related activities that force them to run at full speed all the time.

Still, having a fruitful second half is more than just slowing down or being able to control your datebook. It has to do with a mind-set, an inner compass that is fixed on those things that define the true self. Psychologist Mihaly Csikszentmihalyi spent twenty-five years trying to figure out what makes people happy. He discovered that happiness is not something that just happens. Neither does it have much to do with money, power, or material possessions, as evidenced by the fact that happiness can be found among both rich and poor, powerful and weak. Says Csikszentmihalyi, "People who control inner experience will be able to determine the quality of their lives, which is as close as any of us can come to being happy."

I do not know if Mr. Csikszentmihalyi is a Christian or not, but there is much in the Christian faith that supports his discovery. Our Lord taught us to be like children (carefree), to not worry so much (not be controlled by needs and possessions), and to avoid being controlled by many masters. And in Saint Paul's letter to the Roman church, the apostle explains the importance of controlling the inner being in order to have a fulfilling life:

> Those who live according to the sinful nature have their minds set on what that nature desires; but those who live in accordance with the Spirit have their minds set on what the Spirit

desires. The mind of sinful man is death, but the mind controlled by the Spirit is life and peace.
(Romans 8:5–6)

The irony here is that the church has become one of those masters under which many first-halfers feel hopelessly indentured. The joy that ought to come from serving others in Christ's name is missing because so much of what we do for the church is done out of a spirit of obligation. And that is because, as first-halfers, we have not yet discovered who we are, what we really enjoy doing, and how even the most undesirable task can be a freeing, exhilarating experience if it arises out of our core being. For most people, church work is not a hot fudge sundae, but like the broccoli and spinach your mother made you eat as a child.

Once you have discovered your life's mission, you are in a much better position to regain control over well-intentioned ministry efforts. Instead of dragging your feet to yet another "witnessing weekend," for example, you could decide to allow the light of your faith to shine through naturally by playing bridge every Monday night with colleagues from work. This way, you have regained control in a way that brings together your desire to serve God, your love for a card game, and your need to enjoy a night out with like-minded individuals.

It is encouraging to see how some churches are becoming better at matching passion with talent. Robert Bellah, coauthor of the bestselling *Habits of the Heart*, calls this a function of "mediating institutions." Many churches are adding "volunteer resources directors" or "linking teams" to help people discover how to apply their best selves to invigorating ministry through the church. For example, here in Dallas the Park Cities Presbyterian Church recently launched what they call a Linking Program, which has already developed more than 2,500 different placement opportunities for service. Willow Creek Community Church in the Chicago suburbs has developed a program called Network (now used by many churches nationwide) to help people discern their individual design and to help place them in appropriate volunteer work. Saddleback Valley Community Church in Mission Viejo, California, helps people find their S.H.A.P.E.:

S—Spiritual Gifts
H—Heart, passions
A—Abilities
P—Personality
E—Experience, "know-how"

If Christian second-halfers are to make any progress in seeing their life missions become reality, more and more churches will have to adopt this approach to getting people involved. My own ministry, Leadership Network, has a unit of people working to create the Leadership Training Network, a program that puts on five-day training institutes for volunteer resources directors in churches.

PRACTICAL MATTERS

It is one thing to talk about regaining control yet quite another to really do it. Old habits, even tempered with a brand-new outlook on life, die hard. Here are some things I have done to regain control over my own destiny:

1. *Delegate—at work, play, and home.* You cannot do everything and shouldn't try. This becomes especially important for those whose second half involves keeping their present job but doing it "at half speed." Work smarter, not harder.
2. *Do what you do best; drop the rest.* I tend to be a visionary, so I'm less motivated to do hands-on

implementation, though I can and have done it. Not anymore. Go with your strengths.

3. *Know when to say no.* The more successful you are, the more you will be asked to help others. Don't let others talk you into doing something you don't want to do or don't have time to do; it will become a chore. You want to pursue your mission, not someone else's.

4. *Set limits.* If you currently keep an average of four appointments a day, cut back to two or three. If you normally stay an hour after work, go home on time. If you take twelve business trips a year, cut back to six or eight. Reallocate time to your mission, to your core issues.

5. *Protect your personal time by putting it on your calendar.* I like Ken Blanchard's advice to start your day slow. It is much easier to maintain control over your life if you have a regular quiet time. This time should be more than devotions, though it ought to include prayer and Bible reading. Leave time for absolute silence, for deliberately looking at your life to see that it is in balance. This is probably the most vital activity for me in terms of staying in control.

6. *Work with people you like.* One of my friends, Karol Emmerich, who quit a year ago as treasurer of Dayton-Hudson, says, "I want to find all the people I like being with and find some beneficial work we can do together. In my second half, I want to work with people who add energy to life, not with those who take energy away."

7. *Set timetables.* Your mission is important and, therefore, deserving of your attention and care.

If you do not put your second-half dreams on a timetable, they will quickly become unfulfilled wishes.

8. *Downsize.* When Thoreau moved into a cabin on Walden Pond, he lightened up on the non-essentials in his life. Think about all the time and energy that are drained by owning a boat, a cottage, a second or third car, or a country club membership. None of these things are bad by themselves and are, in fact, designed to provide some fun in your life, but they can very easily become master controllers. Most people I know who own a boat feel they have to use it to make it a worthwhile investment. I also know people who do not particularly enjoy spending four hours on a golf course, but do it because they belong to a club. If these kinds of things stand between you and regaining control of your life, get rid of them.

9. *Play around a little.* Not in the sense that would get you in trouble, but as a way to keep a handle on who's in charge. There is something about skipping out of the office to catch a baseball game in the middle of the week, or taking your spouse to a movie instead of attending a church committee meeting, that reminds you who's calling the shots. Play ought to be a big second-half activity, not so much in terms of time spent, but in importance.

10. *Take the phone off the hook.* Not literally (at least, not all the time), but learn how to hide gracefully. I don't always like talking to voice mail when I call someone, but I wouldn't live without one myself. It lets *me* control who I talk

to and when. Car phones are great because you can call someone when you need to, then shut off the phone and ride in wondrous silence. Unless you're a brain surgeon on twenty-four-hour call, I don't think it's necessary to let people know where you are all the time.

I have also learned, from the wonderful coaching of Peter Drucker, three cardinal principles that guide my work at Leadership Network and help me keep control over my life:

1. *Build on the islands of health and strength.* This is very counter-intuitive for philanthropy, which tends to seek to help the helpless. Building on health and strength, however, is a better idea in that it builds independence rather than dependence.

2. *Work only with those who are receptive to what you are trying to do.* You only have a limited amount of time. Trying to convince people to do what they really don't want to do uses four times the amount of energy required to help someone conceive or implement their own ideas.

3. *Work only on things that will make a great deal of difference if you succeed.*

Desire alone will not allow you to do something new in your second half; you must create the capacity to do it. If you are being controlled by too many time- and energy-consuming activities, you will continue to be frustrated by unfulfilled dreams and desires. Realize too, that you are in unfamiliar territory, and it may take some practice before you feel comfortable. Eventually, however, you will find a way to regain control of your own life.

17

Healthy Individualism

Let's just go ahead and be what we were made to be, without enviously or pridefully comparing ourselves with each other, or trying to be something we aren't.

"The Message," a paraphrase of Romans 12 in *The New Testament in Contemporary English* by Eugene Peterson

I know many people who believe—honestly believe—that giving your life over to Christ and to the church is antithetical to the ideals and character of individualism. They look upon Christians and churchgoers as conformists, and probably mindless ones to boot. In fact, you may have become a little uncomfortable in the previous chapter when I urged you to take control of your life, to become your own master, because as a Christian you have been taught that submission to Christ means "dying to self."

This is a heresy, and a dangerous one at that. In Christ's church, individualism is amplified, encouraged, supported, and complemented. We are each grafted to a body that needs our strengths and compensates for our weaknesses by matching them with the gifts of other members of the body. The image of a weak, wimpy follower is not supported at all in Scripture. Saint Paul urges Timothy to "be strong." He counsels him to "fan into flame the gift of God, which is in you. . . . For God did not give us a spirit of timidity, but a spirit of power, of love and of self-discipline" (2 Timothy 1:6–7). The images Paul sets before Timothy are those of a soldier enduring hardship, an athlete in training, and a hard-laboring farmer—all brawny, manly individuals.

Those who frown on individualism are telling only half the Gospel story. The well-intentioned (and biblically correct) doctrine of depravity is not the whole story. Without God we are, indeed, in need of "amazing grace," but once we are transformed by his grace, we become new, beautiful, and valuable creatures capable of self-love as well as self-control.

I think the reason why so many Christians have accepted the conformist label is that we see so much *unhealthy* individualism in society, especially in the pathological individualism of the "Me Decade" Yuppies, but also in the dipped-in-irony self-centeredness of today's X Generation. This type of individualism (which is not limited to a particular generation, by the way) leads to selfish isolation, alienation, greed, callousness, and guilt. When Jesus talks about dying to self, I believe he is talking about dying to this "me first" pathological self-worship, not the uniquely created self that he has given us.

THE SMALL SELF AND THE LARGE SELF

Much of our first-half misery can be traced back to a preoccupation with self. In the second half, you break free from yourself. While the first-half self is small, the second-half self is large. The first-half self winds inward, wrapping tighter and tighter around itself. The second-half self winds outward, unraveling itself from the paralysis of a tightly-wound spring.

The small self contains only you. It is basically alienated, alone, and pathologically individualistic. The larger self is whole because it is bonded with something transcendent. Self-transcendence has legs; it goes the distance and completes the race.

The Bible relates many instances of the small self. One such example is the parable of the rich fool. Here is a man who had achieved great success, so much that he had to build bigger barns to contain all his treasures. (I see him as a real first-half go-getter, with a house in a pricey subdivision that's too small to hold all his toys.) Yet Jesus called him a fool, saying,

> This very night your life will be demanded from you. Then who will get what you have prepared for yourself? This is how it will be with anyone who stores up things for himself but is not rich toward God.
>
> (Luke 12:20–21)

The rich fool is small and miserly. He is trapped within the little self.

But the Bible is also filled with images of the larger self: the man who knows himself and his mission so well that he will lay down his life for his brother. Think about the Samaritan, whose large self overcame the stigma of doing something out of the ordinary. Or how about John the Baptist who, very much a man who did things his own way, paid the ultimate price for following a cause? And remember the widow who gave out of her poverty, gave everything because she knew who she was and what was in the box?

You too can be a great example if you can make the distinction between your small self and your large self. Sacrificing your immediate self, the small self, for a larger gain is what Jesus meant when he talked about the cost of following him—giving up your tightly wound selfishness to gain something bigger, better. People are at their largest, their most noble and virtuous when they are given over to a cause, something larger than themselves.

INDIVIDUAL TEAMMATES

Each of us is designed by our Creator to be incomplete. As we grow up, we grow from a state of dependence as small children to one of independence as adolescents and adults. Independence feels great, but it is not the final stage. Beyond independence, we have yet to reach the stage of interdependence—the stage where we understand and accept that we cannot accomplish anything significant on our own.

The apostle Paul expresses this best in his letter to the Corinthian church, in which he uses the analogy of the body:

> The body is a unit, though it is made up of many parts; and though all its parts are many, they form one body.... If the foot should say, "Because I am not a hand, I do not belong to the body," it would not for that reason cease to be part of the body. And if the ear should say, "Because I am not an eye, I do not belong to the body," it would not for that reason cease to be part of the body. If the whole body were an eye, where would the sense of hearing be? If the whole body were an ear, where would the sense of smell be? But in fact God has arranged the parts in the body, every one of them, just as he wanted them to be. If they were all one part, where would the body be? As it is, there are many parts, but one body. The eye cannot say to the hand, "I don't need you!"
>
> (1 Corinthians 12:12, 15–21a)

I cannot recall a single thing worth doing that I've accomplished by myself. The individualism in the Bible is the individualism of an eye or a foot—a part that functions as part of a larger, harmonious whole. The individualism so rampant in our culture is a first-half individualism that borders on selfishness; its focus is almost always personal gain. Second-half individualism always finds its strength in concert with others of like-minded vision. I learned long ago to build on my own strength and natural giftedness and to depend on others with complementary strengths to make the work I'm doing complete.

THE SELFISHNESS OF ALTRUISM

Several years ago I had the distinct privilege of hearing a remarkable man who was at that time the world's leading expert on stress. Hans Selye was a microbiologist from Canada who coined a phrase that sounded almost contradictory: altruistic egoism. As Selye explained it, and as I learned more about it from his landmark book *The Stress of Life,* altruistic egoism is nothing more than the biblical truth that helping others helps *you.* Selye had learned that those who earn the goodwill of their neighbors are dramatically better off psychologically and physiologically than those who are looked upon as selfish and greedy.

Selye wrote that the best way to earn the goodwill of your neighbor is to ask either explicitly or implicitly, "What can I do to be useful to you?" And then, if possible, to do it. I can't explain it, but this works for me. And in all the times I have asked this question, I cannot recall a single occasion where someone took advantage of me. Instead, people are stunned by the rarity and vulnerability of the question. And most of the time, I really can do something that is useful, and often it does not require money or very much time.

Fred Smith Sr. told me years ago that being a Christian has to do with learning to do by reflex action that which you first learn to do by duty and discipline. Asking, "Is there anything I can do to be useful to you?" and then doing it is something I learned first by duty. Then, after much practice, it became a reflex action.

For example, I was once in a small group with Jerry Mays, a contractor who was an all-pro linebacker for the Kansas City Chiefs years ago. Jerry was a "gentle giant" who gradually wasted away from cancer with incredible courage and dignity right before our eyes. At one point, I sent Jerry a small lamb and cross sculpture I owned that is a replica of a piece in the Vatican collection. In turn, he sent me one of the most touching and encouraging letters I've ever received, saying that he observed Christlikeness in my behavior. Obviously, the sculpture brought some joy into Jerry's life, but it is impossible to describe the inner joy I experienced in reading his letter to me.

This fleshed out "neighbor love" offers practical, tangible benefits as well. Consider this report which first appeared in the Roman Catholic magazine, *Liguorian:*

> Medical researchers are now finding scientific proof for what Jesus taught so long ago, that giving of self to others is actually a form of receiving (Acts 20:35). This seeming contradiction finds meaning only when seen through the eyes of Christ. Not only are scientists proving this paradox to be true, they further assert that helping others is good for your health. . . . A study done at the University of Michigan revealed that persons who regularly volunteer their time heighten their overall zest for living and increase their life expectancy. Studies on the aging process have reached a similar conclusion. . . . Stress researchers from the University of Illinois found that persons who feel connected with other people are more calm, less tense. . . . Giving can be disguised in many forms, from understanding to empathy, from compassion to acts of service. Whatever it takes, the core is still the same—giving of ourselves is offering love, and love remains the only gift that multiplies when you give it away.

I have read that sometimes people suffering from emotional illness are "prescribed" acts of service or kindness to others because it helps them rise above their own problems. I know this is true because, in the weeks after Ross was lost, I found that the only thing that would bring me "temporary symptomatic relief" (like the promise on the backs of aspirin boxes) was to become mentally engaged in helping someone else. Going out of my way to help someone made me feel better! That is why it is so important to have a cause, a mission, in your second half: not only is it a decoy for your emotional system in order to keep you busy, it is also the key that unlocks the door to your larger self.

I am convinced that part of the secret to a better second half is a proper understanding of self-love. Success in the first half is lonely because it is directed inward. It gains significance in the second half from the "pouring out" of ourselves, our gifts, our talents, our resources. As you begin to hit your stride in the second half pay attention to yourself.

Here are some "road signs" to alert you to your own sense of individualism:

Healthy individualism	Unhealthy individualism
Part of a team	Arrogant and alone
With God (rich toward God)	Without God
Working from your strengths	Functioning in your weakness
Able to confess	Stuck with shame and guilt
Self-realization and community	More success = more isolation = less community

18

Life-long Learning

With all thy getting, get understanding.
An adaptation of Proverbs 4:7
as quoted every month for years
in the back of *Forbes* magazine

I only really became a student after I finished school.
I suspect that is true for most of us. When we were in high
school and college, we were not students, but clients. Education was a means to an end; it provided a union card to
allow us to work in the closed shop of productive life. Public service announcements urge kids to stay in school so
that they can get into college or get good jobs—I do not
recall hearing announcements that told me to stay in school
so that I could learn the meaning of life or an appreciation
for the depth of insight in classical literature.

I am not being critical of our educational system. It
is geared for the first half. We demand that it teach us how
to work, how to have careers, and how to be successful.
For the most part, it delivers; it equips us to be productive.
We do not ask much more of education until we get to halftime, the point at which we finally begin to understand

that life becomes richer when we are students and narrows when we stop learning.

A friend of mine told me about a man he met on a plane who had been in college for fourteen years. He was not a "terminal student," seeking a number of degrees, nor was he in an extended training program related to his career. This man was a mechanic who was being sent by his company to a job at another factory, and had been a mechanic since he graduated from high school. For several years, he welded steel boxes of various sizes together, taking pride in his work. Then he saw an advertisement in the newspaper for a local community college that listed its course offerings, which would be starting in a few weeks. He signed up for a biology class because he liked the outdoors, and he got hooked. He now speaks two languages besides English and has the equivalent of a B.A. degree in English. He has also taken classes in physics, music, religion, and history. And he still welds boxes together.

It would be easy to dismiss this guy as someone who is indulging himself in some nonutilitarian luxury, but something about him appeals to me. Why should all learning have a utilitarian purpose? Why not learn a new language just because you would like to speak and read German or French, not because it is a requirement for a degree or because you need to do business in Germany? This man had discovered the joy of learning, something that he did not discover until after high school. His is a second-half approach to the glorious world of knowledge.

WHY LEARNING IS IMPORTANT IN THE SECOND HALF

There are some obvious reasons why it is important to continue learning in the second half. If learning prepares you to deal positively and productively with change, then it is more important now than ever before. In my brief lifetime, for example, I have seen the treatment of minority groups go from "back of the bus" segregationist policies to the mandated quotas of multiculturalism. You do not adjust to that without learning.

I have also had seven jobs in my professional career, and in my current role as a strategic broker the playing field is constantly shifting. I cannot fulfill my mission unless I am engaged in a fairly systematic, or at least consistent, pattern of learning.

Another reason to learn in the second half is to "unlearn" the doctrine of specialization. Most first-halfers are trained in the language and operations of their particular field. Accountants stay current on tax laws but know little about management theory; a neurosurgeon may have progressed from scalpel to laser to nuclear probes, but would be hard-pressed to treat a gunshot wound. Second-half missions tend to be more holistic and demand a more widely rounded practitioner.

There is also the very practical issue of staying sharp. Senility (not to be confused with Alzheimer's disease) is, I am told, no longer felt to be an inevitable condition of aging. Most gerontologists subscribe to the "use it or lose it" theory when it comes to mental alertness. I have seen too many men and women let their minds grow fallow as they approach their sixties. I do not want it to happen to me, and it does not have to happen to you. Working with Peter Drucker, eighty-four, and Frances Hesselbein during the early years of The Peter Drucker Foundation for Nonprofit Management has shown me what a vital, energetic, and productive season the years after "retirement age" can be.

But perhaps the most compelling reason for nurturing an active mind comes from my admittedly nontechnical interpretation of the New Testament account of Jesus casting out a demon in Luke 11:24–26. Jesus said that when an evil spirit returns to an individual and "finds the house swept clean," it enters that house with even more evil spirits because there is so much room to fill.

I think the key theme here is emptiness, and I don't think it is too much of a stretch to suggest that if we let our minds become empty, they can be filled with much that detracts us from the mission of our second half. One way or another, our minds will indeed be filled with something. I shudder to think what kind of person I would be today if I had given myself a steady diet of talk shows, soap operas, tabloid journalism, and the like. For this reason alone, we ought to be diligent in learning good and wholesome things in order to protect our minds from the debasing things that are so easily absorbed. This is also why I consider studying the Bible to be a valid form of life-long learning. If "garbage in, garbage out" is true, then the reverse must be true also.

WHAT TO LEARN IN THE SECOND HALF

It is impossible to design a curriculum for the second-half student, but I generally apply this rule: You only really learn what you need and are willing to act on; the other is amusement and passing the time away. In other words, you learn best when the subjects you are studying in some way apply to what is important to you.

This rule suggests that the welder I referred to earlier was merely amusing himself, though I have no way of knowing just how he used his knowledge. There is nothing inherently wrong with that—the pure joy of learning could be, for some people, an end in itself. With all the inane things people do to enjoy themselves, signing up for a Spanish class looks pretty good. But if you are learning with no particular goal in mind—whether stated or loosely understood—you will eventually come to view learning as a pastime. I recommend focusing on those things that will help you accomplish your mission, but keeping a creative and liberal view of just what that could include.

For example, I study art. I allow myself to purchase inexpensive art books so that I can cut out a reproduction of an important painting and push-pin it up on a cork board in my closet, where I will see it each morning and evening while I dress. I visit museums and galleries whenever I have the chance, and I have a modest collection of art in my home. I would be hard-pressed to make a direct connection between my study of art and my work as a Christian philanthropist, other than to show that I believe in the power of art to inspire. A Japanese scholar of several centuries ago said, "Great art captures the spirit of a thing." When I look at a painting, I am moved by the beauty or power or emotion of the piece; I learn something about myself and the world—about the human condition. For me, that's enough "permission" to include art in my goal of life-long learning.

Because so much of what I do revolves around human organizations, I also take advantage of seminars, workshops, conferences, and study programs in the areas of business, management, leadership, and related subjects. Likewise, your second-half learning program should include formal and informal learning in areas that represent the "hands on" aspect of your life mission. If you are an attorney and have decided to cut back on work for your firm so that you can provide some pro bono legal counsel to urban ministries, it would make sense to stay current in nonprofit legal issues. Or, let's say you are a public school teacher who has taken advantage of early retirement incentives being offered in many districts, and you feel called to set up a study skills center through your local church. Since you will probably need to recruit volunteers to help staff the center, it might be worthwhile to interview an official from your local United Way or other charitable organization to learn the dynamics of volunteerism.

The mistake most people make when they move into the second half is to rely on good intentions. If, at some point, you become discouraged by lack of progress in your life mission, it is possible that you simply may not have gained the knowledge and information necessary to support your dream.

HOW TO LEARN IN THE SECOND HALF

In many ways, everything that you do in the second half is a form of learning. That is because learning is really just adopting an attitude of discovery. Because of this, expect to learn from everything you approach and don't get too hung up on trying to formalize your study. To show you just how diverse the delivery systems are, I'll list those that have been helpful to me and others:

Formal classroom. Our example of the welder would not be a bad one to emulate. I have, from time to time, enrolled in classes to study something that was either interesting or would help me in my mission. There is a definite benefit to the discipline of a systematic program of study, and the nice thing about going to school when you're in your forties is that the pressure to compete is gone. You already have a job, so instead of pressing to get a grade, you do your best to learn something. In most cases, you'll end up with one of the higher grades anyway (or if you want, you can audit the course and not worry about grades).

Listening and asking. This is probably my most consistent way of learning things. I just ask. Or sometimes I don't have to ask; I'll listen to those around me. If you're a business traveler, you already know how much you can learn (and how easy it is to network) on planes.

Alternative media. All media has a spin on it. If your only source of news is the conventional media (network television, daily newspapers, and news magazines), you'll get a slanted picture—not necessarily a false one, but a slanted one. Instead, listen to National Public Radio and read magazines like *The New Republic, New Perspectives Quarterly, American Demographics, Utne Reader, The Atlantic, The Wilson Quarterly, Wired,* and others. The *Wall Street Journal* and *Forbes* are more than business publications. You may not agree with all of them, but then isn't that part of learning?

Books. Read voraciously and widely, fiction as well as nonfiction. Read Christian and secular books. Form a book study group to gain other perspectives on the book you're reading. Every fall and spring, I participate in a course in the classics with a group of fellow life-long learners.

Tapes. This is probably a holdover from my first-half days, but you can "read" a lot of books while dressing, driving, or exercising. The Learning Company has collected top college lecturers in its "Superstar Teachers Series." Most book publishers produce taped versions of their books. Consult your local bookstore.

Conferences. Well-run conferences can be better than a semester class at a university. Pick up tapes from the sessions you can't attend. Keep the notes and handouts for reference.

Interview people. I am amazed at how easy it is to approach someone and ask for an interview. Once they know you're not a reporter, most people are happy to give you a few minutes. Just make sure you're prepared, and don't overextend your allotted time. They say you are only two phone calls away from anyone on earth. It's true.

Travel. One of the greatest forms of education is travel. Linda and I now make it a practice to travel to and do in-depth study into a different region of the world at least once a year. A new trend among second-halfers is "vacation with a purpose." A trip can combine geography, religion, politics, anthropology, art, and music in one comfortable package.

Television. You would expect this from a guy who worked in television, but I honestly believe that TV can be a great vehicle for learning. I read the *TV Guide* every week and circle those programs that will have useful information for me. I also use an amazing gadget called a VCR Plus to tape programs for later viewing. With the new "information highway" on its way, television will become an increasingly effective tool for learning.

Team learning. Peter Senge says, "Teams, not individuals, are the fundamental learning unit in modern organizations." God seems to have built a governor against arrogance into the design of human beings. We are as interdependent in learning as we are in other areas. After I have thought about some problem by myself for a while, I always find it necessary to enter a give-and-take dialogue with others. It's a way to find the other pieces of the whole puzzle.

One of the great tragedies of civilization is the transformation that takes place in a child's attitude toward learning. At some point in the schooling process, they pass from childlike eagerness toward learning to a passive resistance toward gaining knowledge. Perhaps it is inevitable. What I am proposing, however, is that you really can reclaim an excitement for learning. Second-half excitement for learning shows that you are unashamed to admit you don't know everything, and that you want to learn more. It's acknowledging that "professional" is more of a title or label than a measure of knowledge. In your second half, be willing to become an amateur in a field you haven't mastered.

19

Respect for Externals

All results are on the outside. The inside is only cost and effort.

Peter Drucker

Second-half people are a lot like bassoonists.

Think about it. A bassoonist is not very effective outside the context of an orchestra. Trumpeters, violinists, and pianists can all go solo; the bassoonist, for the most part, cannot. And the few bassoon solos that *have* been written were meant to be performed with an orchestra or ensemble.

If a bassoonist did not accept this reality, he would be frustrated to the point of either quitting or trying to generate some public interest in a solo bassoon performance. Fortunately, bassoonists have generally accepted their lot in life and have provided listeners with countless hours of wonderful music complemented by their distinctive bass tones.

This analogy illustrates two important facts about second-halfers. First, we are secure enough to be team players. And second, we recognize the need to respect externals—to be at peace with those things that we cannot change and that will be with us forever.

My cable television executive team spends about 25 percent of its review time each month looking at external conditions: regulatory changes, changes in customer responses to someone else's offers, changes in culture, new technologies, and demographic changes. We do not waste our time figuring out ways to change those external conditions because we know we cannot. They may become opportunities or threats to our company, but one thing is certain: they will always be with us.

That is not something we learn in our first-half climb. Windmills are for tilting, and tilt we must. Often, the first-half approach to externals is either relentless attack or denial. But there is a fine line between ambition and stubbornness. One of the things that put you in halftime was the realization that you weren't making any headway by constantly butting heads with external conditions over which you had no control.

In the second half, you learn not just to accept the external conditions but to respect them, for it is through respect that you begin to creatively find ways to turn those externals into opportunities. The best example of this is Microsoft, the software maker. Not so many years ago, everyone wanted to stake a claim on the computer mother lode, so companies sprang up overnight and began making computers. And a lot of them made big money. Bill Gates surveyed the scene and saw IBM rising like a huge skyscraper. He knew they would always be the biggest player; that was an external condition he accepted and respected. So instead of aiming his little spear at this huge windmill, he headed off in another direction; and the rest, as they say, is history. Who would have thought that a company worth about one-tenth the value of IBM would one day surpass its value? And what might have happened if Bill Gates had decided to try to build hardware to compete with IBM?

Sometimes the externals are so close they almost devour you. It almost happened to me. I became involved in a venture that took me out of my league, out of my comfort zone. My partner knew that we had to do something to compete with cable and began pressuring me to run some soft porn—actually, it was more hard than soft. I was under a lot of stress because, of course, I did not want to have anything to do with pornography. I was also dealing with the added pressure of running a business that was in danger of failing. You see, the porn might have added new viewers and given us needed revenue, but I refused to allow it. And it was a decision that kept the financial thumbscrews cranked down pretty hard.

I remember trying to teach a Sunday school class in the midst of all this. The lesson was from 1 Corinthians 13, and believe me, I was not feeling like anything that was described in that well-known chapter on love. It must have shown, because afterwards, a guy in the class came up to me and said, "You know, the last time I felt the way you just described, I was a fighter pilot in Korea. Have you ever considered that maybe it isn't work that's getting to you, but the work you're doing?"

He was 100 percent correct. What I needed to do was accept the external reality: I did not belong in that business. I could stay in and fight to my dying day, but some things would never change. So I got out on February 12, 1982, the date that marks the beginning of my second half. It was my big plunge, and I know it was the right thing to do.

THE ROLE OF AUTHORITY

There is no such thing as a life without authority. You can choose the game, but you can't choose the rules.

If you're going to play tennis, you have to serve behind the line and keep the ball within the sidelines. If your sport is basketball, you must dribble the ball up the court instead of running with it. Simply put, when you choose the game, you inherit its rules. And whether you like it or not, the rules govern your behavior. Follow the rules, and your chances of winning are greater. Break the rules enough times and you won't even get a chance to finish the game.

It must have been a first-halfer who said, "Rules were made to be broken." On the way up the ladder, there is always the temptation to skip a step, to take a shortcut. And there is something about submitting to authority that seems wimpy to many in the first half. The reason auto insurance rates are higher for young people is because it has been proven that they tend not to respect the authority of traffic laws. They speed more, take more chances, and tend to fool themselves into thinking they are immune to authority. First-halfers operate in much the same manner. Although outright rebellion is rare, many first-halfers take the "don't touch the stove" warning as an invitation to push authority's limits.

The problem for the first-halfer is this: You need that job to survive. You may not like it, you may not respect your boss, you may not have agreed with the way the company does things—but you can't just up and leave. At least not very easily. Who'll pay the rent and buy the groceries? You are forced, in essence, to accept your employer's authority, even if you don't like it. In the second half, you are generally more flexible; it is easier to make legitimate choices about who and what will be an authority in your life. You will never live free of authority entirely, however—if God is in your box, you have automatically chosen to accept his authority.

The irony of the gospel, of course, is that the more you submit to the authority of Christ, the more radically free you become. This is what makes the second half so attractive to me. I see many young men in their twenties who are struggling so hard to be free of their difficult jobs, tough marriages, and other externals that cannot be changed. I wouldn't want to live that way, and neither do they. When the discomfort level gets too high, they begin asking halftime questions. And once they figure out who's in the box, they realize that they were struggling in vain. The way of the Cross presents us with the greatest and most delicious paradox of all time: to be really free you must submit to God's authority.

I hope that doesn't sound glib or overly "religious." I recognize the fact that even those who are sold out to Christ will face unfair bosses, dull jobs, kids who get in trouble, marriages that turn sour, and a whole host of life's problems. And I do not much care for the "just give it to the Lord" advice that is so easy to dispense. But I will say this: Once you have resolved your first-half issues and have decided that God is in your box, you will have more grace and freedom to live with those problems. They will not disappear; at least, not instantly. But you will be in better shape to deal with them, to learn from them, to even turn them into opportunities for your life mission.

I was a committed Christian when I lost my son. I had already put God in the box and was beginning to implement a mission that made God the primary loyalty in my life. None of that prevented a horribly real external: raging currents can drown even the most powerful swimmer. It was hard enough to deal with that loss, but I can honestly say I do not think I would be where I am today had it not been for my faith. Respect the externals of the natural world and the authority of the supernatural world and it will free you to grow and serve well in the second half.

20

Playing for All You're Worth

> *So choose life in order that you may live . . . by loving the LORD your God, by obeying His voice, and by holding fast to Him; for this is your life and the length of your days.*
> **Deuteronomy 30:19–20 NASB**

Here is a secret you may not want to hear: getting from the first half to the second is not easy. It does not happen in a week, a month, a year. And the lines between the halves are not always clear.

Please don't let that hinder you from playing the game hard. It always occurs to me, when I share my story, that some could get the idea that all they have to do is follow a formula and things will turn out all right. Then, when the formula doesn't work, they get discouraged and resign themselves to the downward slope of their one curve.

I was in halftime for several transitional years, but I still played hard. And I had some fun along the way. You may make some false starts, need to go back and do some more seismic testing, or try another low-cost probe. As I've said before, the key is to start a new curve before the last one peters out.

A friend of mine has one foot in each of the "halfs." He's the managing partner of one of the largest real estate concerns in the world. The debacle of real estate values in the '80s considerably reduced his net worth, so he completely reorganized his company from an asset capital appreciation company to a service company. He has been developing new executives, and, at the same time, he has a parallel career in a number of political and civic concerns—he's on the board of a college and is a very active teacher in his church. At some point I know he will make his parallel career his active one and turn his business over to someone else, like I did. But not now. So he's in the first half, charging full speed ahead to build his company; he's in halftime, taking stock of his life and deciding who's in the box; and he's in the second half, using his talents for a higher cause and working to reorder his life. He may be in all three places for a while longer, but believe me, he's playing hard and enjoying the game.

Remember, the second half is only part of the game. We all have to play the whole game.

I have been asked what sacrifices I have made in my life. It is a hard question to answer because I have most of the elements people seem to want—a vital marriage, lots of time to do with as I please, a successful business. What I think I've had to give up in order to have those things is hours of "doing my own thing." Put another way, I have spent a good portion of my life on either side of the J-Zone in either anxiety, waiting for a deal to go through, or in boredom, enduring the basics of business or of the spiritual disciplines.

I can't count the hours that I have spent reviewing corporate operations, giving managers their time to "show and tell," being an appropriate listener. And, of course, the best news to hear is always the least stimulating: "Everything's okay." I used to listen to Ross intently for fifteen minutes a day, using all the reflective listening techniques I could muster to stay on his train of thought. That may seem like a short time, but it seemed like an eternity when I arrived home with a jumble of "important" things on my mind and a need to relax and be apart from human conversation for a while.

Thomas Merton wrote that all you really need is in your life already. He called it the "hidden wholeness." What he meant was that you do not need to chase after things outside of you to find fulfillment. Even though that's what most of us do in the first half, we eventually learn that money, fame, material possessions, and experiences will never fill us. What we become in the second half has already been invested during the first; it is not going to come from out of the blue.

I used to think that if I ever said a complete yes to Christ, I would become a completely different person—that I would wear polyester and drive used cars, or ride a donkey in an AIDS-infested third world country doing things I had never enjoyed doing. That is not to denigrate those who fit these descriptions, but to point out that they just weren't me. I couldn't figure out why God would equip me as an entrepreneur, conceiver, starter, team builder, manager, and leader and then put me someplace where those things are worthless. I was relieved to discover that God does not waste what he has built. I am the same me I was in the first half, only applied to a different venue.

After God made you, he stepped back and said, "This is a great one!" He planted in your soul a desire to connect with him and then provided a way for you to do it. Whether you're in the first half of your life, in halftime, or playing the second half, God's desire is for you to serve him just by being who you are, by using what he gave you to work with.

21

A 50/50 Proposition

I began this book with my epitaph: 100X. It expresses my desire to be remembered as one who greatly multiplied the seed planted in me by my heavenly Father.

I would like to close with another mathematical formula: 50/50. It expresses my dream for everyone who is en route to the second half.

Several months ago, Sandy Kress, a Jewish lawyer, and Don Williams, a Christian businessman, put their heads together to find ways to improve the Dallas public school system. The schools had been working with test scores, hiring practices, and other technical matters and had seen some improvements. The missing piece of the puzzle was the moral and values dimension. I was part of a diverse, multi-sector, multicultural group Sandy and Don selected who met to wrestle with this thorny issue. Ultimately, we centered our efforts on six different initiatives, one of which was the "50/50 Church."

The basic idea of the "50/50 Church" is to challenge Dallas churches to allocate 50 percent of their resources to themselves and 50 percent to serving their community and world. This may sound like a simple enough idea, but in terms of individuals and churches, it's radical. Most churches feel they are stretching themselves if they spend a tenth of their time, talent, energy, and money on ministry beyond their own congregation. Think of what could happen in your community if every church adopted this 50/50 formula! And think of what would happen to you if you spent half of your time and resources on yourself and your family and the other half on others.

One of the central changes that makes the second half different from the first half is that in the second half the life of faith becomes much more integrated instead of segregated. In second-half living, you will learn that the principle of altruistic egoism is true: doing good to others does just as much good for you. Your life will be a balanced living-out of the gospel; a winsome, attractive, and joyful witness to the fact that life in Christ adds rather than detracts—fills rather than empties. You will have a difficult time marking the boundary between self and others because significance has overshadowed success. Instead of trying to manage the various compartments of your life, you will be your whole self and take great pleasure in all that entails.

Just take a look at the following list of opposing values and attitudes and ask yourself, *Which side do I want to be in during the second half of my life?*

Segregated Life	*Integrated Life*
Personal, private faith	Ministry as part of life
Dogmatism	Paradox
What to believe	What to do about what I believe
Faith means giving up	Faith means addition, abundance, wholeness
We/They:	Us:
That which separates us	That which draws us together

We/They, cont.:	Us, cont.:
Individual sport	Team sport
Independence	Interdependence
Law	Grace
Obligation	Personal choices
External approach	Internal approach
Based on appearances	"As a man thinketh, so is he"
Authoritarian leadership	Servant leader
Sunday Christianity	Seven-day-a-week Christianity
Doctrine-driven	Purpose-driven

The 50/50 church reaches out to serve its surrounding community, living out its proclamation of the gospel rather than imposing an unwelcome ideology on others. Its witness is first by example, then by proclamation. The role of the 50/50 church is to place carriers of faith back into all of the contradictions, tensions, and paradoxes of the community, rather than to isolate people in an unrealistic, cloistered atmosphere for a couple of hours on Sunday morning.

I know I am not the first person to suggest that the church needs to do a better job of interacting with the world. Every believer, I am certain, wrestles with this and truly wants to see the gospel transform our culture. So why doesn't it happen?

I believe the answer lies in individual responsibility. The church will never have credibility in the community at large without *expressed* individual responsibility. People need to *see* our faith, not merely hear about it. When our beliefs are personal and privatized, practiced only inside a building one day a week, we Christians miss out on that glorious opportunity to be salt and light. Worse, I believe that when faith continues to be directed inward, we become one-dimensional, uninteresting, and wholly self-centered persons. We have a work life, a family life, a community life, and a church life. And when segregated like that, each sphere is less robust than it could be.

What does this have to do with your second half? One of the real tragedies of the first half is that people are encouraged to be selfish. No man really wants to put his career ahead of his family, but it happens—the inertia of trying to be successful is just too great for most of us to resist. The third decade of most men's lives is practically a blur, with little time to think through any of the core issues and values that lead to significance. I do not know if this is inevitable; I just know that it happens a lot, and that it almost always culminates in a period of questioning and self-doubt. *Is this all there is?* we ask ourselves. *Do I want to do this for the rest of my life?*

Eventually, your first half will end. The clock will run out. If it happens unexpectedly—if you do not take responsibility for going into halftime and ordering your life so that your second half is better than the first, you will join the ranks of those who are coasting their way to retirement. Your second half will be a slower version of the first, with fewer and fewer successes and very little significance. But if you take responsibility for the way you play out the rest of the game, you will begin to experience the abundant life that our Lord intended for you.

When I look across the Christian landscape in America, I see a powerful reservoir of energy just waiting to be unleashed. I see enough talent, creativity, compassion, money, and strength to transform our culture. I see true believers in every sector of society genuinely concerned about the condition of their communities, but feeling powerless to do something significant to change it.

My life mission, to somehow transform that latent energy in American Christianity to active energy, may seem impossible, but as a bona fide second-halfer, I don't think in terms of the impossible anymore. I honestly believe that I can play a role in releasing the tremendous energy lying dormant in the church—but I also know that I cannot do it alone.

At one point in my halftime, I thought of myself as an arsonist—someone who likes to light fires in people, then sit back and watch them blaze. But the metaphor is not entirely accurate because I really don't like to just sit back and watch. But I do like to light fires in people, and I hope I've ignited something within you, for I believe in every Christian's heart a spark is glowing.

I hope you are feeling the heat of that spark, and that you are growing wonderfully uncomfortable with it.

I hope that when I describe the second half, you begin to feel a breeze blowing deep within; that you are beginning to see what kind of fire you might become.

I hope that as that spark begins to ignite, you get excited, animated; that you start to feel young again; that you begin to dream new dreams.

I hope that as the flames spread, you will realize you can't smother the fire this time; that this is not the puff of good intentions, but a hurricane of commitment.

That is the energy I see when I look into the sanctuaries, Sunday school classrooms, and Bible studies of America's churches. That's the kind of energy I know is within you.

I have concluded that individual responsibility is the key to transforming the church. I can describe for you an effective and feasible program that will position you for significance, but in the final analysis you alone must choose how you want to live. You have the freedom to decide whether or not you want the rest of your years to be the *best* of your years.

My prayer for you is that you will have the courage to live the dreams that God has placed within you.

See you at the end of the game.

Acknowledgments

In the process of working on this book and on reviewing the facts of my life, I discovered a marvelous truth: I have never done anything important outside the context of a team. I think God must laugh at the seeming independence of us human beings who have such a tendency toward hubris and self-sufficiency. This may come from having made a lot of money, earning acclaim in sports, writing a book, or accomplishing something else extraordinary. God finds ways to teach all of us who are puffed up with ourselves how interdependent we really are.

Of all the writing on the interdependence of human beings, I think the greatest is by Saint Paul in the twelfth chapter of Romans where he says,

> Do not think of yourself more highly than you ought, but rather think of yourself with sober judgment, in accordance with the measure of faith God has given you. Just as each of us has one body with many members, and these members do not all have the same function, so in Christ we who are many form one body, and each member belongs to all the others. We have different gifts, according to the grace given us.
>
> (vv. 3–6)

This book and the life it seeks to express are the product of a team. The credit for the book itself belongs most to Scott Bolinder and Lyn Cryderman of Zondervan Publishing. I gave up on the book several times. They didn't. Both made a couple of visits to Dallas to talk the recalcitrant "author" into getting the book done. Lyn Cryderman did the crafting. As well, I am grateful for the writing contributions of Bruce Buursma and Bill Proctor, both of whom helped meaningfully in my effort to get my thoughts into words, and to Rachel Boers for her skillful editing. My assistant, BJ Engle, has spent hours drafting and redrafting the multiple manuscripts. I learned first hand what T. S. Eliot meant when he called writing a "raid on the inarticulate."

I am part of several teams for different purposes. For life planning, Peter Drucker has been the most important person in my life. Early on, when I needed desperately to learn how to manage a business, he was my teacher, as he has been for so many through his books. Later in life, as I entered my second half, Peter became my guide in the shift from success to significance. There are two books in my office: Peter Drucker's large book *Management* as my guide for human things, and the Bible as my guide for spiritual things.

It is enough to have written the book just to carry Peter Drucker's foreword into your hands. It says so much that is priceless to me, but more importantly, so much that is valuable to you. It allows Peter to be your guide in interpreting what is happening, as he has been mine for years.

My first team, of course, is that with my wife, Linda. She is a completely distinct individual, very much unlike me (thank God), but there are times when I can't tell where my thoughts stop and hers begin. I couldn't begin to imagine life without this person whom I love and respect so much. And of course, Ross, my son, whom I lost physically six years ago, is still very much with me. In many ways, Ross was the uncompleted part of my personality—physical, springing with vitality, passionate, a lover of men, women, and hunting dogs. It won't be long in the whole scheme of things until I see him again. We will share eternity together.

I couldn't have embarked on my second half without the incredibly effective operating team at Buford Television, Inc. There's not a better team in cable TV than Ben Hooks, Ron Martin, Tom Seale, Kay Monigold, John Ellis, Dick Green, Arl Cope, Steve Lowe, and the dedicated groups of people who serve our customers under the name Friendship Cable. Frank Burke and Jim Watson have been wonderful advisers.

My brother, Jeff, is the world's best and most supportive equity partner.

Beryl Berry has been my right hand (and that of my mother before me) for over forty years. She knows all the family secrets—the good, the bad, and the ugly. She has outlasted all my other business associates.

Thanks also go to those who provide external capital to our business. My current bank partners are First National Bank in Chicago, Nations Bank in Dallas, Bank of California in San Francisco, and National Westminster Bank in New York.

Civic Broadcasting, headquartered in Jackson, Mississippi, was and is my venture into the civil rights movement in broadcasting. They demonstrate that an integrated and highly cohesive workforce can be achieved in the deep South. Their television stations are number one in each television market where they operate. Frank Melton, with whom I have worked for over fifteen years, is the CEO, and Aaron Henry is the chairman of the board. They do the right thing every time.

The heart, soul, and conscience of Leadership Network is Fred Smith Jr. He is the man Diogenes was looking for with his lamp—the last honest man on earth. Fred, along with the staff of Leadership Network, especially Gayle Carpenter, Carol Childress, and Brad Smith, transform good intentions into reality for the 11,225 Christian professionals on the Leadership Network mailing list and the 1,692 people who have attended Foundation conferences over the past six years. The speakers at these conferences travel great distances and do endless hours of preparation. They are the best in the world.

Paul Robbins, Harold Myra, and Fred Smith Sr. played a pivotal role in the original conceptualization of Leadership Network.

There are a special category of people I call networker/deal makers, who have been very important in connecting me to others. Among them, Doug Coe, Doug Holladay, Don Williams, and Tom Luce have all made major contributions in matching me up with other people.

I am deeply indebted to those who have been my guides through the new, chosen world of what I call the Christian ecosystem in the United States, especially Bill Hybels, Rick Warren, Leith Anderson, Ray Bakke, Gordon MacDonald, Paul Robbins, Harold Myra, Fred Smith Sr., Robert Lewis, Skip Ryan, Terry Taylor, and the indefatigable Lyle Schaller, who just keeps going and going, fresher in his insights than men forty years younger, and ever the optimist.

I am grateful to those who have cast their lot financially with me in my second half. To all those who have become shareholders in the Foundation conferences and who have paid fees and expenses to attend Leadership Network events, I give thanks.

I am part of three small groups: one by conference telephone and two "live." For allowing me to share in their lives, for allowing me to "think my confusion out loud" before them, and for wise counsel that has become an indistinguishable part of my thought life, I want to thank: Don Crisp, Bob Slocum, Don Williams, Bill Breedlove, Fred Currey, Ted Enloe, Jody Grant, Jack Knox, Richard Marcus, Jerry Mays (deceased), Bob Rogers, Bill Solomon, Jim Hoak, Steve Bryant, Doug Coe, Craig Estes, Dee Margo, Matt Martin, Mike Regan, John Snyder, Jim Warner, Jack Willome, Tom Luce, and John Castle.

For all the work we have done together, and especially for serving as shining personal examples, I want to thank the Board of Governors of the Peter Drucker Foundation for Nonprofit Management, which I have been privileged to chair in its early years—Richard Schubert, Sidney Harris, John Jacob, John McNeice. Frances Hesselbein, who has been the founding president of The Drucker Foundation, has been utterly indefatigable in putting the Foundation on the map. She seems to be everywhere at once. Ed Fjordbak of Communities Foundation of Texas and Hedy Helsell of The Center for Nonprofit Management have been great partners in several second-half nonprofit undertakings.

As anyone can tell from reading this book, the advice of Michael Kami has been pivotal and catalytic.

Linda and I have a wonderful network of friends in Dallas and Tyler, the two places we live. We have shared joy and sorrow, birth and death, building up, tearing down, mourning, and even dancing—all those things Solomon mentions in Ecclesiastes chapter 3. To name a few: Peaches and Bruce Brookshire, Marilyn and Frank Budde, Mary Dale and Pat Thomas, Anne and Tom Smith, Nancy and Randy Best, Ann Clark, Merry Jane and Earl Davis, Janie and George Hamm, Donna and Bill Wise, Judy and Don Williams, Pam and Tom Luce, Bess and Ted Enloe.

Ken and Marge Blanchard are great friends and conspirators in my second-half adventures.

Young Presidents Organization and World Presidents Organization have poured hundreds of hours of wonderful education and idea exchange into my life. YPO is the best adult education organization in the world, and for the most part I didn't begin to really learn until I was an adult.

Among those who have contributed immeasurably to my life as spiritual mentors, teaching the Bible and teaching me what the implications of the Bible for my life were to be, are Phil Hook, Shelley Chapin, Dan Russ, Sug Thompson, Doug Coe, Doug Holladay, Howard Butt, the late Ray Steadman, and Alice Mae Harold.

And most of all, I want to presume to acknowledge the partnership of God. It is the unspeakable pleasure, the inexpressible joy of feeling that I am in partnership, little finite me, with the very Creator of the universe. I didn't quite realize this until I read Peter Drucker's foreword for this book. He speaks of a book that is much more than a book that I am capable of writing. I tried, and I couldn't do it. I found it too much for my skills, yet here it is. And for that amazing fact I can only be grateful to God. Good job, God.

Selected Bibliography

Aristotle. *Ethics.* New York: Penguin Classics, 1955.

Autry, James A. *The Art of Caring Leadership.* New York: Avon Books, 1991.

Bellah, Robert N., et al. *Habits of the Heart: Individualism and Commitment In American Life.* Berkeley: University of California Press, 1985.

Bennis, Warren, and Burt Nanus. *Leaders.* New York: Harper & Row, 1985.

Berglas Steven. *The Success Syndrome.* New York: Plenum Publishing, 1986.

Blanchard, Ken, and Norman Vincent Peale. *Power of Ethical Management.* New York: Ballantine, 1988.

Bridges, William. *Transitions: Making Sense of Life's Changes.* Reading, MA: Addison-Wesley, 1980.

Buechner, Frederick. *Telling Secrets.* San Francisco: HarperSanFrancisco, 1991.

Covey, Stephen. *Seven Habits of Highly Effective People.* New York: Simon & Schuster, 1990.

Crabb, Larry. *Inside Out.* Colorado Springs: NavPress, 1988.

Csikszentmihalyi, Mihaly. *Flow: The Psychology of Optimal Experience.* New York: Harper & Row, 1990.

DePree, Max. *Leadership is an Art.* New York: Doubleday, 1989.

____. *Leadership Jazz.* New York: Doubleday, 1992.

Drucker, Peter. *The Effective Executive.* New York: Harper & Row, 1967.

_____. *Managing the Nonprofit Organization*. New York: Harper-
Collins, 1990.

_____. *The New Realities*. New York: Harper & Row, 1990.

_____. *The Post-Capitalist Society*. New York: HarperCollins, 1993.

Frankel, Victor. *Man's Search for Meaning*. New York: Simon &
Schuster, 1984.

Friedan, Betty. *The Fountain of Age*. New York: Simon &
Schuster, 1993.

Gardner, John W. *On Leadership*. New York: Free Press, 1990.

Hagberg, Janet. Real Power: *Stages of Personal Power in Organizations,* Rev. ed. Salem, WI: Sheffield, 1994.

Handy, Charles. *The Age of Paradox*. Boston: Harvard Business
School, 1994.

_____. *The Age of Unreason*. Boston: Harvard Business School,
1990.

Havel, Vaclav. *Disturbing the Peace*. New York: Knopf, 1990.

The Holy Bible, New International Version. Grand Rapids: Zondervan, 1973, 1978, 1984.

Howard, Grant. *Balancing Life's Demands: A New Perspective on
Priorities*. Sisters, OR: Multnomah, 1983.

Hybels, Bill. *Honest to God*. Grand Rapids: Zondervan, 1990.

Johnson, Paul. *Modern Times*. New York: Harper & Row, 1983.

Labier, Douglas. *Modern Madness: The Hidden Link*. New York:
Simon & Schuster, 1989.

Leider, Richard J., and David A. Shapiro. *Repacking Your Bags:
Lighten Your Load for the Rest of Your Life*. San Francisco: Berrett-Koehler, 1995.

Life Application Bible, The Living Bible. Wheaton, IL: Tyndale,
1989.

Muggeridge, Malcolm. *Confessions of a Twentieth-Century Pilgrim*. New York: Harper & Row, 1988.

Nouwen, Henri J. M. *In the Name of Jesus: Reflections on Christian Leadership*. New York: Crossroad, 1993.

SELECTED BIBLIOGRAPHY

O'Neil, John R., and Jeremy P. Tarcher. *The Paradox of Success: When Winning at Work Means Losing at Life.* New York: Putnam, 1993.

Peterson, Eugene. *The Message.* Colorado Springs: NavPress, 1993.

Schaller, Lyle, ed. *Center City Churches.* Nashville: Abingdon, 1993.

Sheehy, Gail. *New Passages: Mapping Your Life Across Time.* New York: Random House, 1995.

_____. *Innovations in Ministry: Models for the 21st Century.* Nashville: Abingdon, 1993.

_____. *The Seven Day a Week Church.* Nashville: Abingdon, 1992.

_____. *21 Bridges to the 21st Century.* Nashville: Abingdon, 1993.

Selye, M. D., Hans. *The Stress of Life.* New York: McGraw Hill, 1956.

Templeton, John Marks. *Discovering the Laws of Life.* New York: The Continuum, 1994.

Willard, Dallas. *The Spirit of the Disciplines: Understanding How God Changes Lives.* New York: Harper & Row, 1988.

Yancey, Philip. *Disappointment with God: Three Questions No One Asks Aloud.* Grand Rapids: Zondervan, 1988.

Halftime is honest and profound. Bob Buford's clear telling of his story and the questions he raises call me to examine my life and declare through words and actions what has ultimate significance. This book is a real blessing.

John Castle, Jr.
Senior Vice President, EDS

Whatever your stage in life, this is a must read. Thoughtful and practical— it will change your life for the better.

Tom Luce
Founding Partner, Hughes & Luce LLP

Halftime is exceptionally relevant to anyone searching to be more useful in the kingdom. It . . . provides the instruction and inspiration to unleash the latent power of God in millions of Christians who are at some stage of mid-life.

Don W. Crisp
President & Executive Director, The Rosewood Corporation

Discussion Guide

Welcome to your journey from success to significance. Across the nation, many readers of the book *Halftime* have gone back and *reread* its contents several times. As author Bob Buford says, "The first time, they are reading my book, but the second time they are reading *their* book." This discussion guide helps you take a more deliberate and more process-oriented approach to the halftime of your life.

While this guide can be used for individual study, ideally, it is designed for study within a small group. Growing into the second half of your life will take more than a desire; a small group provides the essential elements of accountability, discipline, and authenticity, as well as a place to "think your confusion out loud" with people who care about you.

Before using this discussion guide, here are some steps to consider:

Prepare. The questions on the following pages come directly from the contents of each chapter. Before working through the questions, read or reread the contents of the chapter indicated.

Select a leader (in a group context). It's rare that the dynamics of a group work properly unless someone leads it. Prior to each study session, choose someone to guide the discussion, make sure the group stays on relevant subjects, and provide everyone with an opportunity to participate. If possible, rotate the leadership.

Probe for honest questions. Just as a football team gets a break and a pep talk from the coach during halftime, your halftime provides time for reflection. A key ingredient of this reflection is looking deep. Remove any masks or self-doubt and look deep inside yourself.

Encourage accountability. Whether you work through this discussion guide in a group or as an individual, make a point to have one person as an "accountability partner." This person will help "hold your feet to the fire" of accountability. Seek to find a person who will allow you to be honest, yet not judge you. Despite high expectations and goals for ourselves, each of us falls short. But if someone else holds us accountable when we fall off the horse, we can get back on again. Give this person permission to ask questions about progress in your halftime. Often such a relationship is the difference between simply reading the material and applying it to your daily life.

Write down your answers to the questions and assignments. As you work through this discussion guide, take a yellow legal pad or open your laptop and write down your answers to the questions. Or record your answers in your journal. More than simply mentally answering the questions, the writing process will allow for deeper life reflection. Writing down your answers will concretely show your commitment to discover the halftime answers for your life. As the weeks and months pass, you can return to your written answers; they will benchmark the progress of your halftime.

INTRODUCTION: *Opening the Heart's Holiest Chamber*

1. Take a few minutes to consider the end of your own life. How do you want other people to remember you?

2. Bob Buford wrote his own epitaph: 100X. What would you like carved on your gravestone? Think about it for a few moments, then write an epitaph of less than ten words. (Setting a limit on the number of words will help you focus on the essence of who you are.)

3. Categorize the first half of your life. Which of the following elements dominated your life: education, advancement of a career, family, or acquiring physical possessions?

4. How aware are you that the clock of your life is ticking down toward eternity? What in your life right now is going on to make a halftime evaluation exciting and necessary (i.e., family concerns, job success, the waning thrill of the deal)?

PART 1: THE FIRST HALF

CHAPTER 1: *Listening to the Gentle Whisper*

1. Reread 1 Kings 19:11b–12 from the opening page of this chapter. On a scale from 1 to 10, how good are you at spending time listening to the still, small voice of God?
2. What does "having it all" mean to you?
3. Turn to the diagram on page 27. Where are you now in your journey? A spectator, seeker, a follower, a kingdom builder? Bob says that most of us are stuck between first and second base. What concrete steps will move you toward maturity?
4. Have you taken a "leap of faith" into belief? Write down the specific period of your life when you took that step of faith.
5. Think about your life from God's perspective. If God audibly spoke to you about your mission in life, what do you think he would say?
6. Buford raises an intriguing question on page 32: If your life were absolutely perfect, how would it look to you?

CHAPTER 2: *The Hour of Reverse Conversion*

1. Who was your "Mittie Marsh" (page 37)?
2. What have been the turning points for your life? Which events have shaped your career? Your family life? Your social life? Your spiritual life?
3. Think about these life-shaping events. What elements made them significant? The words someone spoke? The actions someone took?

CHAPTER 3: *A Season of Searching and Self-Help*

1. How open are you to change in your life? On a piece of paper, create a scale from 1 to 10. On this scale (1 being entirely closed to change and 10 being the most open), where would you rank yourself?
2. List some of the major changes you've made in the last twenty years of your life (i.e., moves to other locations, career shifts, changes in your management style).

3. Buford says that "a company, just like a person, needs to periodically shift its focus in order to achieve healthy growth" (p. 40). How have you, personally, shifted your focus in the past?

4. As you have gone through the excitement of an advancing career and reaping the rewards of success, what have you lost or left behind as you made gains? Has something important fallen by the wayside?

5. When he was thirty-four, Buford created six core goals for his life (page 43). Make a list of five to ten core goals for the rest of your life. Talk through your list with another person.

CHAPTER 4: *Success Panic*

1. In the opening pages of this chapter, Buford describes a quiet intruder that disturbed his life at the age of forty-four—success panic. Have you hit the threshold where you wondered, "How much is enough?" When did this happen, and what was going on in your life at this time?

2. When Buford reached this success panic, it forced him to address a new set of decisions. Apply the four questions on page 46 to your own life.

3. This chapter makes a clear-cut distinction between "being called" and "being driven." Summarize the difference in your own words.

4. Draw a line on a piece of paper. On one end of the line write success and on the other, significance. Pinpoint where you are on this continuum and make a note of today's date.

CHAPTER 5: *Locating the Mainspring*

1. Draw a box on a sheet of paper. What is the "mainspring," the "one thing," in your life? Write your one-word or one-phrase answer in the box.

2. Instead of just one thing, are there two or three things vying to be put in the box? What sort of confusion or mixed message does this give your life?

3. If you put Christ in your box as your mainspring, what changes will you need to make in your life and career so

that this decision moves from an intellectual decision to a practical application? List at least three, and set a date when you would like to see those changes made.

4. On page 52, Buford says, "It follows the same wonderfully inverted logic as the ancient assertion that it is in giving that one receives, in our weakness we are made strong, and in dying we are born to richer life." In what ways have you learned (or are you learning) the paradox of following Christ wholeheartedly?

5. Now that you've pinpointed your mainspring, what other activities cluster around this choice? What keeps you growing in that direction?

CHAPTER 6: *"Adios, Ross"*

1. When Buford faced the unexpected death of his only son, it shook his comfort zone of life. What recent experiences have shaken you from your comfort zone? In a few words, describe how you've grown through these experiences.

2. In the crucible of life, our faith is stretched. When you have a situation (sickness or death or a rebellious child) that is beyond your control, how do you "trust your way out of it"?

3. On page 58, Buford talks about learning to live as a pilgrim, not in control; as a steward, not an owner; and as a soldier, not with security. Consider the roles of pilgrim, steward, and soldier in your own life. Which area could use some growth in your life? Plan a course of growth to improve in this area.

4. In this chapter, Buford details a simple Quaker prayer that distinguishes between giving and receiving. The prayer incorporates physical action—praying with palms upward to visualize receiving all that you need from God, and then praying with palms downward to visualize leaving your cares in God's capable hands. Turn to page 58, prop the book in an upright position, and then pray the last two paragraphs on the page. Make a commitment to pray this prayer throughout the next week. Then write a sentence or two about the impact that this experience in prayer has made on your life.

PART 2: HALFTIME
CHAPTER 7: *Taking Stock*

1. In this chapter, Buford recommends some key concepts for taking stock of your life:
   a. *Make peace.* What type of regrets do you have in your life? Are there particular people connected to these regrets? List several people that instantly come to mind. How can you make peace with these people through a personal visit, a phone call, a letter, or the mediation of a friend?
   b. *Take time.* The hours and days slip quickly through our fingers unless we create time for what is critical. Write a plan of action to create some evaluation time.
   c. *Be deliberate.* Set an agenda to help walk you through some critical issues in your life. Turn to page 68 and 69 and use these questions as a springboard for your thoughts.
   d. *Share the journey.* Discuss your results with a close friend or a spouse. What insights and possible adjustments did you gain from this person regarding your halftime?
2. Which do you prefer—the hunt or the capture? Why?
3. On page 70, Buford has a halftime drill to help you take stock of the second half of your life. Some of these questions may have already been answered for you in previous chapters. Select four new areas that apply in particular to your situation. Write complete answers to each of these questions.

CHAPTER 8: *What Do You Believe?*

1. Personal belief in a Higher Power is a central concept of *Halftime.* What is at the core of your beliefs? Take a few minutes to think about your belief system, and then list four items that you believe. Start each statement with "I believe ..." (For example, "I believe the Bible guides my life during every day.")
2. How does your personal belief system relate to:
   a. your family   c. your community
   b. your career   d. your private life

CHAPTER 9: *Finding Your One Thing*

1. If you haven't seen the movie *City Slickers,* rent the video. In particular, pay attention to the scene included in *Halftime* where Crystal and Palance discuss the secret of life. What were these men confused about?

2. Many people never discover their "one thing," although they know it is out there somewhere. In the past, what kinds of things have you allowed to temporarily relieve your longing for your "one thing"? (See page 80 for some possibilities.)

3. Have you pursued the dreams and desires from other people for your life instead of your own? List two examples from your past along with the results—positive and negative. Other people can give us input about our "one thing," but the actual discovery will only be found inside ourselves. It is a truth "hidden in plain sight."

4. Think about your uniqueness. With every person he created, God broke the mold. As a unique individual, how do you define your purpose? Buford defines this purpose as "what you do so well that you would enjoy doing it without pay." What is your passion, the spark that needs only a little breeze before it is ignited into a raging fire?

5. How does Peter Drucker define the difference between efficiency and effectiveness, and how does that apply to the process of finding your "one thing?"

CHAPTER 10: *From Success to Significance*

1. What discoveries in your life signaled to you that success wasn't enough? On pages 84 and 85, Buford gives a number of the signals he discovered. Use these ideas to create your own list.

2. Is excellence unattainable? If you have reached excellence, do you feel that something is still missing? If so, what is the missing ingredient?

3. Reread the story of Buford's friend Howard on pages 86 and 87. How have you reacted to friends or business associates who have made these kinds of drastic changes in their careers and lifestyles?

4. Buford says on page 88 that the move from success to significance "begins by stopping wherever you are in the journey to see what's in the box, and then reordering your life around its contents." With an awareness of what is central to your life, what steps can you take to reorder your life around this central focus? What things need to be eliminated?

5. This reordering process for your life doesn't necessarily mean a 180-degree turnaround. How can you make adjustments in your life through gradual changes instead of a drastic reordering?

6. Does the search for significance in your life require you to begin a task that you dislike? Reread the story of the systems analyst on the top of page 89. How can you guard against trying a task for which you are completely unfit?

7. Write the ideal job description for your second-half career or parallel career. What would you have to do to get that job?

CHAPTER 11: *Finding the Center and Staying There*

1. Buford mentions the balance between the frenetic anxiety of the chase and the boredom between deals. As you reflect on the first half of your life, how much balance have you been able to keep? When have you been out of balance? During what period of life was your life in balance? Describe.

2. Laura Nash identifies seven tensions that are common for Christians in the marketplace (page 91). Which of these tensions are familiar to your situation? Which one stands out as most significant in your life?

3. The seven tensions above are "not only necessary but may have some benefits.... You will find peace knowing that you will never resolve the tension." Describe how you are learning to deal with—and thrive among—these tensions.

4. Buford writes on page 93, "Christ meets us, he works with us, in the confusion, in the valley of the shadow of death, in the tunnel of chaos when the familiar landmarks have disappeared." Recall a time when this sentence marked a

reality in your own life. Write God a brief thank-you note for his presence in the confusion.

5. In the final pages of this chapter, Buford tells about a tempting business opportunity—that he turned down. Have you ever turned down a promotion or passed up an opportunity? Why or why not?

CHAPTER 12: *Staying in the Game, But Adjusting the Plan*

1. You may not be able to follow Buford's example of walking away from full-time involvement with work during the second half of his life. How could you take such a leap of faith in your career? Take a few minutes to dream about what your life would look like.

2. What is your attitude about your job? Attitudes can range from "I love my job so much I'd do it even if they didn't pay me" to "I can't stand what I do no matter how much money I make." Draw a line on a piece of paper showing these two extremes. Mark an "x" to show where your attitude is in relationship to your work.

3. Buford says that "the key to a successful second half is not a change of jobs; it is a change of heart, a change in the way you view the world and order your life." Reflect on this statement. In what ways can you modify or adjust your view of the world? How can you adjust or modify the way you order your life?

4. Seismic testing can be a tool to help you restructure the second portion of your life. Enlist the help of two friends or spiritual leaders (who you can easily reach) whose counsel you value and trust. Make an appointment with these friends. When together, ask: "In your opinion, what can I do to be useful?" Then listen carefully and write down their responses.

5. As Buford says, "You cannot operate out of a strength that God doesn't give you" (page 102). Write a sentence about what you perceive you could do best for God.

6. With the information from the previous question about what you do best for God, how could you engage in some

low-cost probes? List three things you can do to gain hands-on experience that combine your gifts with service to God and the church. Which of these could be developed into a new career? How?

7. Perhaps you are considering your second-half career, yet you like your first-half job. How could you take a half-speed approach to your career?

CHAPTER 13: *Overlapping Curves*

1. Study the graph on page 108. Then face the fears listed at the bottom of that page. Which, if any, of these predominate in your life? Maybe your fear is something completely different. If so, write it down and focus on this aspect of your halftime.

2. How can you continue a pattern of constant growth through use of overlapping curves (page 109)? Where are you on the curve in the important segments of your life (work, relationships, spiritual life)? Using the overlapping curves principle, plan a practical course of action for yourself.

3. Turn to the list of ideas for the Sigmoid Curve on page 110. It's more than just changing; it involves selecting the right time to make a shift. How will you know when it's the right time?

4. What impact will retirement have on your second-half career? How you can avoid the caution from Peter Drucker in this chapter: "Retirees have not proved to be the fertile source of volunteer effort we once thought they would be. They cut their engines off and lose their edge." What would have to happen in your life to be fully engaged in a "parallel career" within the next ten years? If you are interested in developing a parallel career, list specific steps necessary and a date for completing each step.

CHAPTER 14: *Leaping into the Abyss*

1. On his desk, Buford has a plaque that states, "On a mission for God." Imagine your own plaque with a motto important to you. What would it say?

2. While the first half is all about gaining, which sometimes results in loss, the second half is more about releasing and relinquishing, which usually results in strength. List three to five things you will have to release and relinquish to move into your second half.

3. Maybe you're beyond the mid-forty limit which Buford discusses for halftime. What encouragement can you gain from the statement, "Anyone who has grown weary of his or her life can do something to change it for the better" (page 113)?

4. As you consider moving into a second-half career, what makes you hesitate? Write down three specific barriers to a second-half career, then identify ways to overcome those barriers.

5. Take some time for self-reflection. Is now the right time for you to develop a second-half career? When would you like to jump into the abyss? What do you learn from the stories of Jim and Jack in the final pages of this chapter? Write down a key principle from each story. Then consider how it applies to your life.

PART 3: THE SECOND HALF

CHAPTER 15: *Life Mission*

1. Reread the personal mission statements on page 121 (Andrew Carnegie) and page 122 (Bob Buford). Then write your own in a sentence or two.

2. On page 123, Buford details a number of life commitments. What are your commitments in life? List seven different areas, using this list as a catalyst for your own ideas.

3. Peter Drucker suggests two important questions to discover your unique role in life. What have you achieved (competence)? What do you care deeply about (passion)? Write your responses to these questions.

4. Focus on defining your life mission. Schedule some time to write your life mission statement using the last two paragraphs of page 124 as your guide.

CHAPTER 16: *Regaining Control*

1. Reflect on your current schedule and daily events. Is there room in your "cup of life" for anything new? List four items that you may need to change or eliminate in order to recapture some time.

2. Each person has economic and social capital (page 126). How do you spend your economic capital? How do you use your social capital? After answering these two questions, examine both lists. Do you need to convert some of your economic capital into social capital? Make some concrete plans for change.

3. Buford writes, "The second half of life is about regaining control of your life—about calling your own shots." He gives the example of Peter Lynch and his career shift. If you are unable to control your work life, what potential major losses could you encounter in other important areas of your life in the years ahead?

4. More than controlling your date book, regaining control involves a mind-set that is fixed on your true self. As psychologist Mihaly Csikszentmihalyi said, "People who control their inner experience will be able to determine the quality of their lives, which is as close as any of us come to being happy." On a scale of 1 to 10, how would you evaluate your control of your inner experience?

5. Write three ways in which you can you apply the adage "work smarter, not harder" to your present job situation.

6. Are you able to say no? Some people are better at this skill than others. If this is a personal struggle for you, keep a journal of various tasks or projects that you have said no to or simply not volunteered to take on. Use this list as an encouragement or growth step for your future.

7. Look back at your daily planner for the previous three months. How much time each week was devoted to your personal time? How could you modify your daily schedule to give yourself more personal time?

8. Reflect on your coworkers and colleagues. Do they zap your energy or enhance it? What changes can you make to surround yourself with people with whom you enjoy working?

9. Are your possessions draining you physically and emotionally? How could you downsize in order to regain some control of your life and resources?

10. Think about the telephone. Many of us have learned to dread its shrill ring. How much does the telephone dominate and control your life? How can you "learn to hide gracefully"?

11. List three things you like to do to have fun. Approximately what percentage of your time is devoted to each one? Is this enough time, just right, or too little? What can you do to make it just right?

12. Reread the three cardinal principles that Buford learned from Peter Drucker (page 135). Which of these three principles are you implementing well? Which ones could use some adjustment in your own life? Plan a course of action to strengthen the weak principles in your life.

CHAPTER 17: *Healthy Individualism*

1. Turn to the illustration of small self and large self on page 138. Which one describes you best? How can you sacrifice your small self for the larger self?

2. How would you categorize yourself and your career? Independent? Dependent? Interdependent? Buford defines interdependence as, "the stage where we understand and accept that we cannot accomplish anything significant on our own." What practical steps can you take to move toward interdependence?

3. As you've begun to understand your life mission, how can this mission help others? List two ways in which your new mission will be an aid to others.

4. Think about the road signs that mark the difference between healthy and unhealthy individualism. (See the chart on page 145.) Reading through this list, are there areas where you can

improve? Map out a strategy to implement change in these areas during the next several weeks.

CHAPTER 18: *Life-long Learning*

1. Would you call yourself a life-long learner? Think back over your education. Do you regularly learn new material with a level of excitement, or are you rather narrow in your approach to acquiring new information?

2. Examine what you've written about your life mission. How are you engaged in a fairly systematic pattern of gathering information related to this goal?

3. How much have you specialized in your learning patterns? Think about your career. Have you narrowed your expertise or broadened it through the years? What steps could you take to become more of a generalist instead of a specialist?

4. How do you select what to learn during this life-long learning pattern? Buford suggests a simple rule: "You learn best when the subjects you are studying in some way apply to what is important to you." Think about what new information you've been absorbing lately. Is any of this material not relevant to what is important to you?

5. Is your system for learning diverse enough? On pages 149–152 Buford gives a number of different delivery systems for learning. Rate your use of each of these delivery systems with the following guidelines:

    a. need more
    b. need less
    c. just about enough

6. Identify one of the above areas in which you would like to see improvement. Write a brief plan for using this delivery system to learn more.

CHAPTER 19: *Respect for Externals*

1. How is a second-half person like a bassoonist? Finish this sentence: To become a bassoonist I need to ...

2. Evaluate the externals in your life. List some of the factors that you can't change that will be with you forever. Do you accept and respect these externals? As Buford says, "It is through respect that you begin to creatively find ways to turn those externals into opportunities."

3. How could you turn the externals that you can't change into opportunities? Consider what happened to Bill Gates at Microsoft (page 154) or the pressure put on Bob Buford to air pornography on television (page 155). How can you apply lessons from these stories to your own life?

4. How do you handle the role of authority in your life? As Buford writes on page 156, "Whether you like it or not, the rules govern your behavior. Follow the rules, and your chances of winning are greater. Break the rules enough times and you won't even get a chance to finish the game." How can you apply this maxim in your own life?

5. How have you submitted your dreams and plans and desires to the authority of God? Buford writes on page 157, "To be really free you must submit to God's authority." How is this paradox of submission a reality in your own life?

6. List two problems or difficulties in your life. Through your relationship with God, how are you discovering the grace and freedom to live with those problems? (Consider the balance that you've found between the externals of the natural world and the authority of the supernatural world.)

CHAPTER 20: *Playing For All You're Worth*

1. How are you avoiding the syndrome of keeping a foot in each half?

2. Consider where you are in the game of life. Are you playing the whole game, or just the first half? What are some of the sacrifices that you've confronted during the game?

3. Reflect on what Thomas Merton meant by the phrase "hidden wholeness." How have you found this to be true in your own life?

4. Saying yes to God doesn't mean that you will have to work in a third-world country or an occupation that you don't like. Think about the fact that "God does not waste what he has built." How does this shape your thinking about what it means for you to follow God as you discover your second half?

CHAPTER 21: *A 50/50 Proposition*

1. What does Buford mean in the opening pages of this chapter when he uses the formula 50/50 to express his dream for everyone en route to the second half? Explain this concept in your own words.

2. Look over the list of opposing values and attitudes on pages 162–163. Consider the difference between a segregated and an integrated life. On which side do you want to live during your second half? Where are you now?

3. How is your faith in God actively incorporated into your daily life? More than simply handing out tracts or talking with people about the Good News, what evidence can people *see* regarding your faith rather than hearing about it?

4. Reread the last paragraph on page 164 where Buford recounts his vision for the Christian landscape. How can you capture this energy in your own life? What steps are you taking to unleash it?

5. Buford says that "individual responsibility is the key to transforming the church" (page 165). Consider your local church. What role and level of responsibility are you taking to change it?

6. Throughout the process of discovering your halftime, what prominence has prayer had your daily life? How are you finding the courage to pursue the dreams you've received from God?